Ottakar's LOCAL HISTORY *Series*

Carmarthen

PLAYER'S
Nº 3
EXTRA
QUALITY
CIGARETTES
WOODBINE
-the
great
little
cigarette
Player's
Please
ADMIRAL
CAPSTAN
TIPPED CIGARETTES
GIFT STORE
BRISTOL
PLAYER'S
cigarettes
CIGARETTES
GET YOUR
Player's
Please
HERE
T. LLOYD

Dark Gate.

Ottakar's LOCAL HISTORY *Series*

Carmarthen

Compiled by
Dominic Williams

First published 2002

Tempus Publishing Limited
The Mill, Brimscombe Port,
Stroud, Gloucestershire, GL5 2QG

British Library Cataloguing in Publication Data.
A catalogue record for this book is available from the British Library.

ISBN 0 7524 2670 2

Typesetting and origination by Tempus Publishing Limited
Printed in Great Britain by Midway Colour Print, Wiltshire

Contents

Pump House, Quayside, now demolished.

Foreword

'O! Call back yesterday – bid time return', pleaded the incomparable William Shakespeare in *Richard II*. It was sound advice, and it's precisely what Mr Dominic Williams and his collaborators have sought to achieve in this delightful book. We are all aware of that world which we have lost, but here we are given an opportunity to regain it – partly at least. True, life was physically more demanding fifty to a hundred years ago, but the community was much more closely-knit then, and the human relationships were warmer and more forthcoming. Reading this volume I was impressed by what excellent memories its authors have and how interestingly they regale us with their stories. Characters and situations come vividly to life in this miscellany of captivating recollections from times long gone by. I warmly commend it to all those who enjoy nothing better than time-travelling to earlier phases of Carmarthen's long and colourful past.

Professor Sir Glanmor Williams
University of Wales
Swansea

Rhagair

'O! Call back yesterday – bid time return', oedd ple yr anghymarol William Shakespeare yn ei ddrama *Richard II*. Cyngor doeth oedd hwnw, a dyna'n union at beth yr anelodd Mr Dominic Williams a'i gydweithwyr yn y llyfr deniadol hwn. Gŵyr pawb ohonom faint a gollasom wrth i'r oes o flaen fynd heibio, ond dyma gyfle inni ailymafael ynddi – yn rhannol, beth bynnag. Mae'n wir fod bywyd yn gofyn llawer mwy oddi ar ddynolryw yn gorfforol hanner canrif neu ganrif yn ôl, ond yr oedd y gymuned yn ymglosio'n nês yr adeg honno a'r gydberthynas rhwng pobl â'igilydd yn gynhesach a pharotach. Wrth ddarllen y gyfrol hon, rhyfeddais at gof gafaelgar ei hawduron ac mor ddifyr yr adroddent eu hanesion. Daeth cymeriadau a'u helyntion yn fyw o flaen fy llygaid yn y casgliad cyffrous hwn o atgofion 'slawer dydd. Fe'i cymeradwyaf yn frwd i bawb sy'n ymserchu'n arbennig mewn teithio trwy amser yn ôl at oesoedd cynharach gorffennol maith a lliwgar hen dref annwyl Caerfyrddin.

Proffeswr Syr Glanmor Williams
Prifysgol Cymru
Abertawe

Welsh language road sign.

Introduction

It was planned that this would be the first book in the series that was bilingual. Contributions were invited in English and in Welsh, and there are included both translations and pieces in Welsh or English alone. In my editing role I prioritised the preservation of the author's voice, therefore any colloquialisms or grammatical constructions that are dialectal have been left in the text. This is particularly true of the Welsh language pieces, as the Welsh language is crucial to the identity of Carmarthen. It has become apparent, even during the course of this modest venture, that Welsh is primarily an oral language, in day-to-day use, but in writing still represented best by its poetic voice. A great example of this is the piece entitled *Ysbyty Dewi Sant,* which contains elements of Cynghanedd.

The articles in this collection are wonderfully diverse and eclectic, befitting the range of authors who have submitted them. We were honoured to have a forward provided by Professor Sir Glanmor Williams, very possibly the greatest living Welsh historian. Submissions were received from published academics, noted historians and local people who'd never before dreamt of putting pen to paper. All are worthy of inclusion and indeed the diversity and range of work adds to the interest of the book.

Some material considers the contrast between myth or legend and reality when considering the earliest origins of the town as well as in a more modern context through local folklore and ghost stories. Historical pieces range from medieval times to the last decades of the twentieth century. Institutions that provide health care and education are analysed by articles written from different perspectives. Overall I hope my selection gives the sense of a market town that acts as a living heart for surrounding rural communities.

Many young people who have left Carmarthen and returned recently, for visits, have commented to me that the town is becoming much more lively and interesting than they remembered. This bodes well for the future of the town. The articles collected in this volume recall days when people were less likely to leave Carmarthen, but rather benefit from, add to and create a local community. Local projects help raise the awareness of the importance of a sense of community and shared history. Local history societies have produced works of popular history that further inspire others. Many people also work locally on living history projects such as the Gwili Railway. There are many people I would like to thank for the education they have given me, so many that I needed a full page for acknowledgments. It has been both pleasure and a privilege for me to be involved in the publication of this volume.

With so many worthy entries to consider I focused on variety to provide an account of Carmarthen's local history as fascinating as possible. To this end I have been forced to omit, (because of the limitations of quantity rather than quality of work in my remit) pieces of work of equal value to those included. We can only hope that based upon the performance of this publication we already have a core for Volume Two!

Dominic Williams.

Acknowledgements

Many thanks to: Ottakars and Tempus Publishing, Caroline and Huw Charles-Jones of Brawdy Books for much advice, Sinead Murphy for long hours typing, Dianne Williams for support, Noel King, Friends of Carmarthen Archives Society, particularly Margaret Evans, David Cook and John Davies (County Archivists), Eilenud Rees and Llansteffan local history society for direction, Beti Davies, Dyfed Family History Society, Menter Bro Myrddin for translation, Sir Glanmor Williams for telling me history was about people telling their stories, Dewi Thomas of Carmarthen Library, Chris Delaney of Carmarthen Museum, Sian Morris for much rescue, Mike Richards for inspiration, Emma Morris for knowing all of Carmarthen, and all the contributors, those published and those kept for next time, for teaching me so much.

Dominic Williams.

Contributors

Mike Benbough-Jackson
Heather Chambers
Dr John Crane
Idris Davies
John Davies, Prize Winner: 'Penycae'
Marion Davies, Prize Winner: 'Rees Davies'
W.L. Davies, Prize Winner: 'Growing up in Carmarthen'
Janet Dube
Andrew Fyall
Margaret Griffiths
Russell Grigg
Rebecca I. John
Dr Caroline Jones
David L. Jones
J. Towyn Jones
Pamela Jones
Nest Lloyd
Victor G. Lodwick
Eiluned Rees
Aurelia Reynolds
Don Smith
Susan Sorek
Jenny White

1 Origins of a West Wales Capital

Carmarthen bred

'Carmarthen Market? Oh! That's easy. Follow the main road from Newcastle Emlyn into Priory Street, turn right at the Old Oak and go straight on. You can't miss it'.

'The Old Oak?' 'Yes. It was originally called Merlin's Oak'.

I resolved to discover something of Merlin's origins and background. Inevitably, fact and fiction blur together, as, particularly in early accounts, historians glean a great deal of their information from hearsay, much of it oft repeated and, sometimes, misrepresented. And so it proved in my researches on Merlin, as he appears in a bewildering spectrum of sources. Many of these attribute the first reference to this possibly fabled character to Geoffrey of Monmouth, writing in *The History of the Kings of Britain*, published in 1136. However, he may have evolved his tutor to the boy Arthur and, later, advisor to his Kingdom, from a prophet mentioned in *Historia Brittonum* by Nennius and in the prophetic poem *Armes Prydain* in the early tenth century. Even earlier, in the *Annales Cambrian* for the year 573, some two generations after the entry for Arthur, is recorded simply '*Merlinus insanus effectus est'*, meaning 'Merlin is effectively insane'.

To Geoffrey, however, is given the credit for his name. He was born in Caer-fyrddin, eventually known as Merlin's City, today's Carmarthen. He was the illegitimate son of a monastic Royal Princess of Dyfed, one of a sisterhood of nuns, who lived in St Peter's church, and was initially called Emrys or Ambrosius. The Latinised version of 'Myrddin' would be *Merdinus* but Geoffrey made it *Merlinus*, as the former appellation might have suggested to his Anglo-Norman readers the vulgar French word 'merde', meaning 'excrement'. His grandfather was King Meurig ap Maredydd ap Rhain, a sub-ruler of the Demetia region bordering on Ceredigion.

His prison and/or burial place is said, variously, to be beneath Merlin's Mound at Marlborough College in Marlborough (Wiltshire), at Drumelzier in Tweeddale (Scotland), Bryn Myrddin (Merlin's Hill) near Carmarthen, Le Tombeau de Merlin (Merlin's Tomb) near Paimpont (Brittany) and Ynys Enlli (Bardsey Island) off the Lleyn Peninsula.

Numerous novels, poems and plays centre around Merlin. In American literature and popular culture, Merlin is perhaps the most frequently portrayed Arthurian character.

There are many references to him in the famous *Black Book of Carmarthen*. Written by a Welsh-speaking monk of the Augustinian Priory of St John in the town around 1250, it is the oldest known manuscript in the Welsh language, containing a priceless collection of early poetry. It is now in the National Library of Wales at Aberystwyth. In it, in verse form, are recorded *Myrddin converses with Taliesin*, the latter yet another luminary of ancient Welsh literature; *Merlin's Appletrees* and *The Ohs of Merlin*.

Geoffrey of Monmouth also wrote *The Prophesies of Merlin* in 1151. They outnumber

Merlin.

even those of the later Gaelic prophet, the Brahan Seer of the Scottish Highlands. Coinneach Odhan, who died in 1577, had 'the gift of sight'. Among his prophecies were the Battle of Culloden, the Highland Clearances and the coming of the railway. How many of Merlin's forecasts have come true is difficult to establish, as so many were allegorical in nature. Among the prophecies on his native Carmarthen is the best known, 'When Merlin's oak shall tumble down, then shall fall Carmarthen town.' The stump of the tree, embedded in concrete held together with iron bands, has long disappeared. How often has the town been flooded since?

Andrew Fyall.

The King of the Ravens

In 1984 during excavations at Friars Park, off Lammas Street in Carmarthen, a fragment of a leaded stained glass window was unearthed. The fragment was tentatively dated to 1250-1280, making this piece of leaded window, with the possible exception of a small piece from York Minster, the oldest surviving piece of medieval window lead in the whole of Great Britain. Within the leaded window was a piece of stained glass depicting the outline of a bird, the head and body occupying one quarry and the wings two quarries on either side; the bird was etched in black paint on a red ochre background. The bird, a raven, was the emblem of the Urien Rheged, the sixth century King of Rheged, legendary knight of King Arthur, from whom a prominent Carmarthen family traced their descent.

The site is now occupied by a Tesco store but in medieval times was the home of the largest Franciscan friary in Wales. The friary was founded during the reign of Edward I; the earliest reference to Carmarthen's friary was in 1284. However, after the Dissolution of Monasteries by Henry VIII in the 1530s, the friary fell into disuse and deteriorated rapidly. By the twentieth century nothing was visible of the friary building and it was only when the Dyfed Archaeological Trust excavated part of the area, in response to the proposals for the building of the Tesco store, that the full extent of the impressive building was brought to public attention.

King of the Ravens, Friars Park.

The friary contained the tombs of many illustrious persons, including Edmund Tudor (father of Henry VII), Guffith ap Nicholas, Sir Thomas Rede, Sir Rhys ap Griffith and Sir Rhys ap Thomas. Only the fate of two of the tombs is known; Edmund Tudor's tomb was removed to St David's Cathedral and can still be seen today. Sir Rhys ap Thomas resides in St Peter's church, Carmarthen. Three generations of the same prominent Carmarthen family rested here. Griffith ap Nicholas, his son Sir Rhys ap Griffith and grandson Sir Rhys ap Thomas. Griffith ap Nicholas traced his descent to Urien Rheged and adopted the symbol of the three ravens on his banner.

> 'With the famed ravens of the son of Urien of old' (1)

Griffith and his family played a significant role in the century after 1430 during the troubled period of the Wars of the Roses, when opposing factions, Yorkists and Lancastrians, struggled for dominance of Britain and the Crown. West Wales in particular had been resistant to Yorkist power. In 1461 the Battle of Mortimer's Cross witnessed the execution of Owen Tudor, the grandfather of Henry VII, and allegedly Griffith ap Nicholas, grandfather of Rhys ap Thomas. The fate of the Lancastrian adherents was finally settled at the Battle of Tewkesbury in 1471, and affected the two prominent families of West Wales whose fortunes were to be inextricably linked.

The heir to the Lancastrian claim, the young Henry Tudor, with his uncle Jasper, was exiled from his home at Pembroke castle to France, not to return to Wales until 1485. The young Rhys ap Thomas, with his father Rhys ap Griffith, went to France also, prior to the Battle of Tewkesbury, to the court of Burgundy in voluntary 'exile', returning sometime in the 1470s. However the family fortunes and prestige

> 'had been curbed and its position neutralised'. (2)

Yorkist rule was now imposed upon Carmarthenshire and Cardiganshire.

It was the fate of Rhys ap Thomas to elevate the family fortunes once more, this time however to reach greater heights than could have been imagined by his grandfather.

Rhys ap Thomas and Henry Tudor were approximately the same age; Henry was born in 1457 and according to the *Archaelogia Cambrensis* so was Rhys, although it seems more likely he was about seven years older than Henry. Both had been in France and may well have met there, perhaps it may have been an inevitability that their paths would cross again.

In 1485 Henry Tudor made a bid for the English Crown. Henry's return had been prophesied and the prophecy implied that he was seen as a returning Arthur leading the Welsh to their rightful position. But prophecy did not supply the means to achieve these ambitions. Henry needed real support and the backing of powerful Welsh lords. One such man was Rhys ap Thomas, Lord of Carew. On his return from France, Rhys had carefully set about increasing the family fortunes and had raised himself to an influential position in Wales. He had also raised his own force of well-drilled men. It was this contingent of men, which according to a contemporary English ballad comprised 'eight thousand spears', that Rhys led to meet Henry when he landed at Dale, near Milford Haven on the 7 August 1485.

Rhys had received favours from the Yorkist King Richard III in 1484. Richard had granted him an annuity of forty marks a year, the first Yorkist favour to have been granted to the family since 1462. The growing threat to Richard from Henry Tudor sought the King to seek support from the Welsh lords. The King also took the precaution of requiring these lords to take an oath of allegiance, and in Rhys' case added the stipulation that Rhys' young son, who was about five years old at the time, would be held as hostage. In response to this Rhys agreed to guard Milford Haven as instructed to prevent Henry Tudor from landing but pleaded for his son to be returned.

When Henry Tudor finally landed on 7 August 1485, with a ragged army of exiles numbering 2,000, many of whom were suffering from the sweating sickness later to spread through and decimate the troops, Rhys was there to meet him. Legend has it that Rhys, in order to keep his oath to Richard 'that Henry Tudor would only enter Wales over his body', lay underneath Mullock bridge and allowed Henry to pass across. However, Rhys did still not openly declare his allegiance to Henry, in fact he may have only done so when Henry had reached Shrewsbury. Both of their armies, Henry's and Rhys', made their way by separate routes through Wales, meeting probably at Welshpool on 16 August when Rhys finally declared himself for Henry.

The Battle of Bosworth in Leicestershire on the 22 August 1485 was a major turning point in British history.

Rhys ap Thomas was one of Henry Tudor's leading commanders; with approximately 2,000 men under his command, pressure was soon successfully exerted upon Richard's battle line. An indication of the military attributes and capabilities that Rhys held.

However, the supreme accolade that Rhys achieved in the battle was striking the blow that killed Richard. Guto'r Glyn in his praise poem says, 'killed the Boar (Richard), destroyed the head.' (3)

This is also partly confirmed by a Burgundian writer Jean Molinet, who records that it was a Welshman who delivered the fatal blow to the King with a halberd when Richard's horse got stuck in the marshy battlefield. (4) The end of the Wars of the Roses heralded in a new golden age under the Tudor dynasty, and Rhys ap Thomas had played a crucial part in helping to establish it. Rhys was dubbed a knight bachelor three days after the battle by the new king Henry VI

'And today is declared a knight,
And his raven and his shield-line by line,
To Harry the king power is long given'.(5)

Rhys was present at the new King's Coronation in Westminster Abbey on the 30 October and became a trusted and loyal member of the King's council. Within a couple of years he had become a knight of the body in the King's household. Henry valued Rhys for his standing and power in South Wales, particularly in the West, and as early as 1485 the King had taken steps to ensure that Rhys' public authority in the region was enhanced considerably. By the 6 November that year Rhys had became Chamberlain of South Wales. This appointment was for life and gave Rhys the control of the wealth and resources of Carmarthenshire and Cardiganshire.

At this time Carmarthen was the largest town in Wales and the headquarters of the King's administration. Rhys was mayor of the borough on four occasions. He became steward for life of the lordship of Builth; in fact his power and influence in south and central Wales were unrivalled.

His military talents were also employed by the King, both at home and abroad. When the war with France began in 1492 Rhys was among the first to assemble his retinue at Winchester to cross the channel and besiege Boulogne. It was Rhys that the King chose to help his come to an agreement with Charles VII at Etaples that enabled the English and Welsh armies to withdraw on terms that were decidedly advantageous to them.*(6)*

The death of the King's uncle, Jasper Tudor, on 21 December 1495, was a further turning point in Rhys's career. Rhys was appointed justicar of South Wales and on the death of

St Peter's church.

William Devereux, later in 1502, constable of Aberystwyth castle. Henry's trust in Rhys never diminished over the years, he affectionately called him 'Father Rice' in deference to his wisdom and wise counsel.

On a personal level the King chose him to oversee the building of a tomb for the body of his father Edmund Tudor, Earl of Richmond. Henry assigned £43 10s 0d from the clerical subsidy of 1496-7, collected from the archdeaconries of St David's and Cardigan for, 'the making of a newe tombe for our most dere fadre', and part of an annual gift of alms to the Grey Friars church in Carmarthen where Edmund had been buried. The marble tomb can still be seen today in St David's Cathedral, where it was taken at the time of the Dissolution when the friary was abandoned.

In 1499, on St George's day, Rhys was finally elevated to the peerage and received the Order of the Garter from the King. To celebrate this great honour, festivities were held at Carew Castle in Pembrokeshire, one of Rhys estates. Few such events are known of having been organized in this period, so this must have been a very significant and splendid occasion, mirroring the events taking at the actual ceremony in Hereford.

In 1509 the new King Henry VIII succeeded the throne. The links between Rhys and the Tudors still remained strong, for Rhys' son had been a member of Prince Arthur's household (Henry VIII's elder brother). Rhys remained in the forefront of events and Henry VIII found, as his father had done before him, Rhys' military skills invaluable. There was only one incident that marred the glittering career of Rhys and that was his implication in the murder of Gruffyd Rede *(7)* the constable of Carmarthen Castle in 1509. The post of constable was the only position Rhys had been unable to attain and was much coveted by him. Nevertheless William Thomas was appointed as constable and Rhys was given the stewardship of Pembroke Castle instead.

During his later years Rhys devoted his time to running his estates and one can only guess at the wealth that he had built up for the family over the years. The family fortunes were sadly to be lost by his grandson Rhys ap Gruffyd whose unsuccessful plot against Henry VIII caused the family fortunes to be ruined in 1531.

By 1525 however, Rhys health was failing, he died in the summer of that year and was laid to rest in the monastery at Grey Friars. Rhys ap Thomas was the last of the great chivalric heroes of the medieval period, as Iowerth Fynglwyd said of him while he was on a visit to the Kings palace of Sheen: 'It is unlikely that nine Saxons would give in Sheen/ A challenge to the Raven of Harry the King'.(8) Rhys household had been considered 'One of the most important cultural centres in Wales'. He had held virtual autonomy in South Wales for nearly fifty years, indeed he was King of Carmarthen in all but name. Rhys ap Thoams could be considered to be Carmarthen's most illustrious citizen, a proud and noble man worthy to carry the banner of the ravens of Urien. Those ravens had soared high, yet within less than ten years after Rhys' death, his grandson had fallen victim to the Crown and the monarch whose ancestor rested there dissolved the Grey Friars monastery. Sir Rhys ap Thomas' tomb was removed to St Peter's church in Carmarthen, where it can still be seen today.

Almost 500 years from the date of the Battle of Bosworth the 'Raven of Harry the King' made its reappearance in the stained glass window found in the Friary excavations, perhaps to serve as a memorial to the town's 'King of the Ravens.'

Susan Sorek

Endnotes

1) Lloyd, Arch. *Camb. Fourth series IX,* (1878), p 202-6.

2) R.A. Griffiths, *Sir Rhys ap Thomas and his family,* (1993), p 37.

3) I. and J. Lloyd Williams, eds., *Gwaith Guto 'r Glyn,* (1939) p 263.

4) J.A. Burchon, ed., *Chroniques de Jean Molinet II,* (1848) p 409.

5) W.A. Shaw, *The Knights of England II,* (1828) p 23.

6) Hay, *Polydore Vergil,* p 52.

7) C. Lewis, 'The Literary Tradition of Morgannwg', in T.B. Pugh, *Glamorgan County History, Vol. III: The Middle Ages,* (1971), p 449-554.

8) Jones & Rowlands, *Iowerth Fynglwd,* No. 7.

2 Rural Life

Once the site of a cottage called Lainfach

Penycae: A farm above the fields

Prize-winning entry

At last I found the place I was looking for. I was six miles from Carmarthen, on a long narrow road near Felingiom, when ahead of me I saw the patch of trees. It is now a wilderness but once there was a cottage here – a cottage called Llanfach.

As I stood there on the roadside, peering through the trees, I wondered if some ruminants of Llanfach might still be there, hidden beneath this greenery.

My father was born here a hundred years ago. He was the second son of John and Miriam Davies and they called him David after Miriam's father.

Llanfach was already overcrowded. There were already eight in the family – my grandparents John and Miriam, their two children, Elizabeth and Denial, and also John's four children with his first wife Rachel – Thomas, Jane, Sarah and Jemma. Now with David there were nine.

My grandfather, then forty-five, did not intend to stay forever in Llanfach. For twenty years, while working hard for others, he had been longing for the day when he would have his own farm. Just one year later his dream came true and he was given the tenancy of Pen y cae. It was a thirty acre farm about half a mile away with eight small fields, set on a slopping hillside overlooking Felingiom. Penycae belonged to Sir John Dillwyn Llewelyn, whose local agent had, it seems, decided that John deserved his chance.

My father was not yet two when they moved to Penycae, but in his later years he could still remember how he made that journey – sitting in a barrow, pushed by his brother Tom or by one of his big sisters. First they went up the road to Felingwm until they reached the lane that lead to Penycae. This bumpy lane was not easy for a barrow or a cart but in the end they reached the farmhouse, their new home.

On a recent visit I was surprised to find that in the eighty years that have gone by since then, the outside of the house has hardly changed at all. The rooms inside the farmhouse were not huge, but in the living room downstairs there was, my father said, a table big enough for all the family to eat together. Above the mantle piece there was hanging in pride of place a big, framed photograph of Daniel, my grandfather's only brother and his family. Many years before they had left Wales and sailed across the sea to Salt Lake City. The parlour was not often used. William the youngest son, who died when he was only five, was laid in here until the funeral at Sittim – and so was Miriam when she died in 1931. The young ones were not usually allowed to use this room and my father could not take his books in there. If he wanted somewhere he could read there was another place to go. He often climbed his favourite tree quite near the farmhouse until he reached a place where he could sit and there he would spend hours among the leaves. This tree became known as Denial's tree.

When they first came to Penycae the house had no back door and the kitchen left a lot to be desired, but then the workmen came and these faults were both corrected. The new

The house at Penycae, 1920.

Photograph taken in Carmarthen before leaving for Salt Lake City.

kitchen pleased my grandmother, whose skill in cooking was well known.

If you needed water for the kitchen, that was clean and crystal clear – you took a bucket to the well just round the corner. If the fire was burning low there was a pile of logs not far from the back door or you cold fetch some coal from across the farmyard.

There were no callings in the bedrooms when they moved in. When you looked up from your pillow you could see the slates above you. But then one day the carpenters arrived and chopped down some trees. They dug a deep saw-pit and with a long two-headed saw they made the beams they needed. And before long they left, and the bedrooms all had callings.

During this time two babies were born upstairs at Penycae. William in 1904, a third son for John and Miriam, and then on Christmas Day in 1907 a second daughter Eunice, who was the last addition to their family.

At Penycae, as in many smaller farms, the farmyard was directly in front of the house. It was an important place. The cows were gathered here ready for milking. Carts were loaded and unloaded. Horses were shod and a hundred jobs were done.

My father had a painful memory of an accident that happened here one hot September day. His mother was going to the dairy with a bucket full of boiling water. She had nearly crossed the farmyard when she heard somebody shout. So she put the heavy bucket down and went to see what the matter was. But just a moment later David arrived and, wanting to cool down, he plunged his hands into the water. Miriam heard the cry of pain and she came running, but the damage had been done. My grandfather rushed off to fetch a relative who was a healer. On their way back they picked some hedgerow plants – one of them succulent with thick fleshy leaves. He used these to make a soothing cream which took away the pain and the damaged skin began to heal.

Beyond the farmyard there was a line of buildings, which together were bigger than the farmhouse; the parlour, where the cows were milked, and the dairy, where the milk was

The barn used as a workshop shown beyond the farmhouse.

Sittim.

taken, a stable for the horses and some storehouses for the crops that were gathered in. A barn in which the cart and all the farming tools were kept and a workshop where my grandfather did his woodwork. There he made gates and fence posts, and sometimes new beehives for the garden.

There were eight fields at Penycae. They were on the hillside above the house: Ca'Fry - the upper field, Ca' 'warty – the field above the house, and Cae Bach – the little field. Near the house there was Ca' Ydlan – and the granary field and Ca Wyn, the field of lambs. There were three more fields below slopping down towards the tree: Y Waun – the meadow, Ca' Canol – the middle field and Ca' Pensarn – the field above the road.

They did not often have to leave the farm to shop for food. So for what reasons did they go beyond its boundaries? If there was a tool that needed mending or a horseshoe that had to be replaced, that meant a visit to the blacksmith in lower Felingwm. Sometimes a sack or two of grain was taken to the mill for grinding and sometimes a visit was made to the village shop to post a letter or to buy some salt and sugar.

From time to time a longer journey was necessary to a pit some miles away to fetch some coal. On Saturdays they sometimes net to the market in Carmarthen when they had butter, cheese or eggs to sell and perhaps some clothes to buy.

When the children reached school age, they made their way each weekday morning into upper Felingwm. They began by walking through two fields – Ca' Ydlan and Ca' Pensarn. After crossing the stream that was the boundary they walked along a path to Troedyrhiw Felda, and there they joined the road into the village. At teatime when my father was coming back from school Cora, his father's dog, was always waiting for him by the stream and then they would walk or run together through the fields – back home for tea.

On Sundays the family all walked to Sittim, the Baptist chapel in lower Felingwm. This

Lunch-break on the Harvest Field, Penycae, 1924.

The Brechfa Road Express. The proprietor was Daniel Davies.

was a longer walk than the one to school and it was made twice, sometimes three times, each Sunday. At Sittim they met their widely scattered neighbours and caught up with the news. On winter nights when they walked back from Sittim after the evening service it could be very dark. People who have always lived in the towns do not realize how dark a country road can be. Sometimes my father said if the skies were clear the stars above would shine in a spectacular display to help them on their way. When they were back at Penycae, and the lamps had all been lit, the first job to be done was cleaning the mud from their best boots and clothes so that they would be all ready for the following Sunday.

The author's father.

It was not an easy task bringing up a large family on a thirty acre farm. By selling their surplus my grandparents needed to make money enough to pay the rent and to buy these things they could not grow or make or do for themselves. They therefore aimed at making the farm as self-sufficient as it could be.

In food they almost achieved this goal. Their meat, fruit and vegetables, their milk and eggs all came from the animals and fields of Penycae. Wheat could be taken to the mill in Felingiom and returned as flour. In the dairy my grandmother made cheese and butter and in the kitchen she baked the bread and made a wide variety of puddings, pies and cakes. In the autumn she made jam and from the beehives at the bottom of the garden came enough honey to last them through the winter. Among the few food stuffs that they had to buy were things like sugar, tea and salt.

The woodland on the farm was enough to supply their log pile by the kitchen door – but the coal had to be brought from a pit some miles away. Their clothes and boots were bought mainly in Carmarthen, but my grandfather had the useful skill of making clogs, wooden soles for leather boys which made these boots last longer.

Sometimes my grandfather needed other people's skills – those for example of the slaughterer and the vet – and sometimes it was necessary to pay for these. Wherever possible however the farmers in the area would exchange their skills. My grandfather was an expert in woodworking and also in the building of round hayricks. If another farmer had a special skill he needed then an exchange might be arranged. Neighbouring farmers also helped each other with the harvest.

One day in the autumn the annual rent was taken to Carmarthen. Sir John Dillwyn Llewelyn invited all his local tenants to a rent dinner at one of the local hotels in town, the Ivy Bush hotel on Spilman Street. When you arrived you took your net to a side room where a steward sat with his big ledgers, which listed every farm. The celebrations followed – good food, plenty of drink, cigars to smoke and good friends to meet again. This dinner was a high spot in the year. Once, to his regret, my grandfather had to miss this occasion and my father, then in his teens, went in his place. When in returned to Penycae he had a handful of best cigars to give away.

My father always recalled his childhood at Penycae with gratitude and pleasure – but it is perhaps significant that neither he nor his elder brother Daniel chose to take up farming. Why did they turn their backs on Penycae? Partly perhaps they had seen what a hard life it could be. The farmer of a thirty acre farm like Penycae could not afford to pay wages of a labourer. All the labour needed had to be their own. There were the things that had to be done each day whatever the weather and whether they felt well or ill. My grandparents accepted this without complaint and I admire them for it.

Which of my sons will help me on the farm when I grow older?' This was the big question for a farmer of a thirty-acre farm. In many cases it was the youngest son who stayed at home to help his parents.

At Penycae a third son, William, was born in 1904 and my grandfather perhaps felt that this question had been answered. But sadly things did not work out that way. In 1909 William fell ill and died when he was five years old. The big question had to be asked again, who now would be the son who would stay at home to help them. Would it be Daniel – or David, who was now the youngest?

My father, David, won a scholarship to the grammar school in Llandeilo and then a place at the University of Wales. Once farmers' sons had always followed in their father's footsteps, but times were changing and both Daniel and David had been attracted by other occupations. It was their youngest daughter, Eunice, who in the 1920s helped my grandparents at Penycae. Bu when Miriam died in 1931 my grandfather decided that it was time to call a halt. He sold his stock, gave up the tenancy and went to live first with Daniel and then with Sarah at Llanarthney. She was the only daughter of his first family who still lived nearby. Eunice, now free to choose her occupation, became a nurse and went to live in England. My grandfather died in 1933 at Sarah's house – not far from Paxton's Tower. He had worked hard throughout his life. Not all his dreams came true but in his final years I

Eunice in 1932.

hope that he remembered the good times at Penycae and his achievements there.

Almost a hundred years has passed since John and Miriam Davies moved with their family to Penycae. The lane you go down from the road is as bumpy now as it was then and on the outside of the farmhouse it looks the same. Eunice their youngest daughter died a year ago at the age of ninety-three- but their family has grown and now includes another three generations.

When I am at Penycae I can travel back through time to meet people I have never seen and those whom I now miss. Some places have a touch of magic. Penycae has this for me.

John Davies.

Bygone days

Countrymen of an age will possibly have happy memories of volunteer villagers helping a local farmer with his hay harvest and pitching tumps of hay onto a horse-drawn 'gambo'; a flat-bottomed Welsh hay-cart, with the loaded hay growing ever higher and extending well beyond the framework of the cart and over the horse's back until only the horse's head and neck was in sight.

Their reward was an ample supply of cider or home brewed beer, a convivial harvest supper and a load or two of farmyard manure for their garden.

Many of the older generation of farmers and farm workers will remember how they helped neighbouring farms at thrashing and sheep shearing times when extra help was needed. They were in a sense social occasions, where farmers and farm workers worked together, ate, chatted, and joked together. They were in many ways the good old days, and even though they were working days, they were happy convivial occasions.

Sadly with the arrival of the combine harvester the need for a gang of men working together around a threshing machine are but memories, while sheep-shearing has with few exceptions, been taken over by peripatetic gangs of New Zealand styled shearers and even native New Zealander shearers. Today, working on a highly mechanized arable or dairy farm is a lonely and unsociable occupation.

Farms generally have got bigger while farm workers are fewer. Stock farms have become more intensive and factory-like. It could be argued that mechanization and modernization is progress, while there are many who would condemn much of modern day intensive animal farming as being inhuman and uncaring.

What a contrast to the days when even small farms were blessed with a host of workers. Most certainly for many it was a happier way of working and living. On many farms young women were employed to help farmer's wives who catered for the men who worked on the farm and the young women who not only worked in the farmer's house but on dairy farms were employed making butter and cheese and even helping with the milking.

There was a time when many Welsh farm workers, regardless of whether they were 'living in' or not, were fed by the farmer's wife. This was not an accepted practice on the English side of the border or on the larger Welsh farms. The term 'two tables' was used to describe a situation where the workers were fed on a table set apart from the farmer and his family. On some farms it was in the same room while on other farms the workers ate in a completely separate room that was commonly called the 'Table room'. Eating on some farms could also mean that the food that the workers were fed differed from what the farmer and his family ate.

I will never forget being asked by a young farmer, whose parents were away on holiday, to advise him regarding an implement that he was having trouble using. As it was a nice evening I took along my then young wife and my tractor driver who was an expert on the machine in question. Having resolved the problem we were invited into the farmhouse for supper. The farmer's son, a man in his mid-twenties, was accompanied by his farm worker, who I considered to be a pleasant and sensible man. I will never forget when we sat down to eat, three of us sat with the young farmer at the 'Masters table', while the young farmer's employee sat in isolation at the 'Workers table', which was only a few yards away. It was unbelievable!

Reflecting on the evening's experience, I could just picture the young farmer and his worker, two men of roughly the same age the 'young master' and the 'servant boy', sitting and eating at their separate tables, even when his parents were away! It was like a scene from a Charles Dickens story.

Visiting craftsmen were also a part of the farming scenario. They provided an essential service to pretty well all but the large estate farms, who would have employed their own specialist tradesmen.

The saddler would arrive at a farm carrying a satchel containing his basic tools: his needles and awl, wax and thread, a half moon knife, pricking wheel and punches, tacking hammer and tacks etc. He also took flock or sheep's wool for stuffing and renovating worn collars, cart saddles and riding saddles. A 'stitch in time' could save precious time! A poor or rotten harness was a danger to man and animal.

A horse collar or cart saddle worn and misshapen would need re-padding, if a horse was not to end up with a sore shoulder or blistered back, which would make a valuable animal unworkable and useless. A maimed animal couldn't work but it had to be fed and cared for, and was in effect a costly encumbrance while a seriously maimed animal could end its days in the 'knacker's' yard.

There was always work for the saddler. A stitch in time could even avoid replacing an expensive piece of harness. In response to a request by the farmer's wife, a saddler would even refill and renovate a worn horse-hair mattress that had lost any semblance of its original shape, or make or repair a leather bag or some other item.

There were not many years when horse drawn vehicles were commonly used by farmers that wheelwright's didn't pay a working visit to most farms. My own recollections are of my father's favoured wheelwright arriving at our farm with his bag of well cared-for tools, having walked for a few miles from the neighbouring village. He was a master craftsman who with his adze alone would sculpt the most elaborate of designs, depending upon the type of vehicle that he was working on. It could vary from making or repairing a sturdy working 'tip-cart' that was used mainly for carting loads of manure or lime for spreading on the chosen fields, or it could have been the 'Gambo', a traditional Welsh hay cart that needed some repairs prior to the coming harvest. Or a light cart or float which was the equivalent of a modern day farmer's light van or Land Rover and trailer, and used for carting sheep or pigs or other goods to market or elsewhere.

The more affluent would also have had a trap or a gig that would in a way equate to a latter-day farmer's saloon car. Horse-drawn vehicles were designed and made to meet a farmer's specific needs. Possibly the most skilled part of the wheelwright's work was repairing and replacing the decayed parts of cartwheels and making new wheels. To band their wheels, wheelwright's generally required the services of the local blacksmith. In his forge the wheel's steel band was heated almost to red heat to expand it before it was placed over the wooden rim of the wheel. Then, as the heated steel tyre cooled and contracted, it tightened and clamped the spokes into the hub and the outer wooden rim of the wheel.

If the contracted steel tyre was too tight, the parts of the wheel could buckle and the wheel-wright's time-consuming work would be ruined.

With a well-grounded farmer a wheelwright would be able to select timber that in many cases came from trees that had been felled on the farm, sawn up into planks or into balks by a local sawyer, before being stored to cure, high and dry on beams in a barn or some other suitable building. Well-seasoned steel hard oak, elm and ash were the essential materials needed for the wheelwright's craft. It was important that the wheelwright used timber that was well cured and would stand the test of use and time!

Wheels were designed to suit a specific vehicle and whatever it was used for. A vehicle that transported heavy loads needed wheels that were strong and stout enough to support a heavy workload. Conversely a light cart or trap with its strong but lighter wheels was designed to carry its lighter loads at a faster pace on roads. The hub of a wheel was usually made of elm, the spokes were made of oak, while the felloes, the curved sections that form the rim of a wheel, were made from ash. Ash was considered to be more springy and resilient than the other native timbers.

I'll never forget seeing Dai Saer, our local wheelwright, patiently and manually sawing inch by inch and foot by foot through steel hard oak, which not only went to show the industry of the man but the quality and temper of his tools. He was a man of few words, but the one thing that would rouse him was anyone handling or getting too near to his precious tools! I well remember that this was often the case when my inquisitive young toddler brother wandered into the cart-shed where he usually worked. He soon learnt that he wasn't welcome anywhere near the artisan's tools.

Williams 'Tyncoed' was what you might call a lay animal doctor. He most certainly was called upon to 'doctor' sick animals, castrate colts and ram lambs and dock the tails of cart horses.

He started his working life as a horse-drawn ambulance driver, which is probably where he acquired his basic knowledge and skills.

In early summer, before the inevitable thundery 'blowfly' weather, Tyncoed, as he was commonly called, was kept busy docking the spring foal's tails, gelding mature colts and castrating the new season's ram lambs and bull calves.

Docking was a barbarous and bloody operation where the practitioner used a guillotine-type of instrument to sever a part of the horse's tail. To seal and stop the bleeding the vein ends were cauterised with a hot iron. Even today I can still sense and relive the smell of the singed flesh and the sizzling sound of the hot irons on the poor animal's bloody veins!

At one time a short stubby tail was an accepted characteristic of heavy cart horses (Shires) and carriage horses. Thankfully the bestial practice was made illegal some years ago. The only good thing that could be said about a horse with a docked tail was that it made the job of passing the tail through the croupier, which was an essential part of a cart horse's harness, easier; while in the summer with horses grazing on lush grass it made the task less messy for the horse's handler!

In his castrating role, seated with his legs astride a bench, and with his clamps, searing irons and castrating knives, and his specially concocted panacea for all ills, consisting I believe of green vitriol (copper sulphate) and pure pigs' lard, set out along side him, he would studiously castrate the ram lambs and the bull calves as they were held upturned and facing him on the bench. Following each operation he liberally dressed the wounds with his green vitriole ointment. Stockholm tar was also used to ward off the maggots of the dreaded blowfly! When required he also castrated male piglets.

The end products of the castrated ram lambs and young bulls were considered by many to be a gastronomic delicacy, depending I suppose on just how highly you rated your sweetbreads!

Gelding all but aspiring stallions continues, but today the operation is performed by veterinary surgeons who, instead of using secretive healing ointment concoctions, use antibiotics.

Even today a veterinary surgeon would consider the implication of the maggot-producing bluebottle weather. Hot, thundery weather was not a good time for castrating!

While 'Tyncoed' was our bacon-butcher, from time to time he was also called upon to deal with an animal that had met with an untreatable accident. Unfortunately in the pre-freezer days the only option with a large casualty animal was that hopefully a butcher might be tempted to take the animal and offer some compensatory payment. With a small animal, such as a lamb or a calf, the meat could at least be shared with friends.

From my early childhood, my recollection of Sid was of a person who would arrive sometime in the autumn or early winter. Having spent the previous evening renewing old acquaintances in the village pub, arriving at our farm in the dead of night he'd spend the night sleeping buried in the hay that was stored in the loft over the cows. The following morning, having washed and shaved, he would proclaim his arrival at the breakfast table.

Following his usual Saturday out and possibly one or two too many ciders in the local, as a young boy it was often my job to discover just where Sid had burrowed, and wake him up! I never knew his surname, but for years he was a regular visitor. During his, you could say sojourn, he spent his time hedge-laying and he was a master of his craft.

Good hedges were essential to a mixed stock farm. Sadly, today countless hedges have been ripped out to make fields bigger and more suitable for modern-day farming machinery.

I believe that he was a Somerset man who had probably moved to South Wales like so many other immigrants in search of work. If Sid had a problem, it was not tied to his ability as a hedge-layer, it was that his only solace came from a pint or so of cider. For all his funny yet sad ways, with no home or family that I knew of, he was always quite clean and respectable. There was a time, especially in the nineteenth and the early part of the twentieth century, when bands of itinerant pieceworkers moved about the country seeking work.

Manual workers were always in great demand. 'Navvies' as they were known helped to build the canals and gangs of men were required for building and servicing the roads and the railways. Men were also in demand on arable farms at critical times for hoeing and harvesting. Gangs often worked on a piecework basis. When they were paid they invariably found a public house where, apart from sorting out their wages, they also found at least some comfort as well as spending their hard earned wages; and they had to find somewhere to shelter and sleep! They slept rough, often in a farm outbuilding or some other basic form of shelter. They were never encouraged to sleep anywhere near hay or anything that might be flammable.

Thankfully gone are the days when gangs of men tramped the country penniless, looking for work. Maybe Sid had at one time been a member of a tramping gang.

David L. Jones.

Following in the family footsteps

I live in the house where I was born, No. 4 Brook Cottages, Llansteffan. The cottages were named after the open brook that ran through the village past our row of cottages. We had to cross little bridges to get at our front gates. It was a very pretty brook and the village lost some of its character when the brook was filled in. Next to the cottages is the parish church, where I spend nearly as much time as I do at home, not that I mind, because I think of the church as another home. I can't remember when I first went to church, because my parents would have taken me there as a baby. My father, William Arthur Taylor, was a motor mechanic and he worked in a garage near the quay in Carmarthen, on a site now part of the police station premises. My mother, Lucy Evelyn Taylor, was a housewife. They had come to live in Llansteffan in the late 1920s. I had an older brother and sister, Peter and Joan.

I have seen many changes in Llansteffan, and in the house too. Some are for the better. It's very nice to have electricity and running water and central heating, things I didn't have in the early years of my life. On the other hand, we have to lock our doors now and children can't wander all over the place as we used to. We were never afraid to go out playing in the fields or up the castle or down the beach.

The church has to be locked, which is a great pity. Even people who are not regular church-goers used to like to pop into church to sit quietly and perhaps say a private prayer. Visitors miss being able to go inside the church, which is very old and has interesting wall-paintings and fine, stained-glass windows. Often visitors have some connection with the village; they would have spent holidays here as children or their parents or grandparents are buried in the churchyard.

My parents are buried in the churchyard. They were very faithful members of the church, never missing a service from choice. All of us children had to go to church on Sundays, to the morning and evening services, and to Sunday school. We sang in the choir and joined in any weekday activities connected with church. My father was verger, churchwarden and Captain of the Bells. My mother sang in the choir and was an active member of the Mothers' Union. But she did all sorts of other things as well, unglamorous things like cleaning the brass and scrubbing the floors. The floors needed a lot of scrubbing when the churchyard paths were just hardened earth. She washed and starched the church linen and mended anything that needed mending, including the kneelers. She was a wonderful needle-woman. She took flowers to church and would go to a lot of trouble arranging them. Some of the flowers were from our garden, but we also went out and collected wild flowers from the hedges. Every Easter we walked up Plas Hill to look for primroses which were made into a cross.

In the last few years I have been verger, sacristan and churchwarden in our parish church. I am often in the church on my own and memories come flooding back. During services I used to sit where the children's corner is now. Taking toys and books to amuse children was unheard of when I was small and my only distraction during sermons was looking at the two stained-glass windows nearby, in memory of the Scott and Parnall families. I could describe them in detail with my eyes closed. Their various duties took my parents to church when there were no services and I was used to sit watching them at work until I was old enough to help. It is only now that I really appreciate how much I learned by watching and helping. The duties of a verger and a churchwarden haven't changed all that much since my dad's day. The biggest difference is having to set the alarm system!

There have been big changes in the church generally. Congregations are much smaller and fewer young people come to church. At one time there was a vicar and a curate in Llansteffan, and the churches of Llanybri, Llangynog and Llangain each had its own vicar. Now Llansteffan shares a vicar with Llanybri, and Llangynog and Llangain share a vicar with Llanllwch. Also, we have a lady vicar, the Reverend Siân Jones, who is also the Rural Dean. Women priests were not thought of in the old days. The chapels are even worse off than the church. Moriah (Methodist) and Bethany (Baptist) are still going, but neither has a Minister. Bethel (Independent) has closed, but the mother-chapel, Capel Newydd in Llanybri, has survived, although without a Minister.

Of all the jobs I do in church, the one that gives me most pleasure is being in charge of the flowers. For the big church festivals, I organise a team of people for thematic arrangements, with each member of the team being responsible for a window or a particular area. It gets a bit chaotic at times, but we have a lot of fun. There is a roster for providing flowers for Sundays, but a lot of those who give flowers ask me to arrange them. I often think of my mother as I am doing the arranging. Fashions change in flower-arranging as in everything else and I try to keep up to date by reading books, going to flower festivals and talking to other flower-arrangers. Little did I think when I was fetching and carrying water for Mam's containers that I would some day be doing arrangements for weddings and flower festivals. We had a big flower festival for the Millennium, depicting aspects of village life through the ages. It fitted in with a village pageant and an exhibition.

The church bells were restored in 1998, after being silent for about thirty years. The restoration was paid for with generous donations and a grant from the Central Council of Bell-Ringers under the Ringing in the Millennium Scheme. It was a memorable day when they came back after restoration. The lorry bringing them was decorated and was parked for a time in Guildhall Square, Carmarthen, and the St Peter's bells rang a peal in celebration. There were loud cheers when the lorry came into view in Llansteffan. Llansteffan Square was packed with people, many in Victorian costume, with Des Cridland in his mock mayor robes and chain. The atmosphere was much the same on Millennium night, when we rang in the new Millennium and the whole village was out on the square hugging and kissing. None of us will ever forget it. By that time I had followed in father's footsteps and become captain of the bells. He would have been very proud. Dad died very suddenly in 1970. He called in the doctor's surgery in town one morning, the doctor told him to go home and rest, he returned to the garage to tell his colleague, Mr Gowman, who said he would run him home. While Mr Gowman was putting his tools away, Dad collapsed. It was the police who brought the news to our door. It was a terrible shock.

I think I am more like my father than my mother. Certainly I haven't inherited Mam's skills as a needle-woman. But I can use a fork and a spade like Dad. We always turned over the garden together. Like most other people in the village, we grew our own vegetables. We kept chickens too. It isn't all that long ago that I gave up my chickens. They found a good home with Aurelia Reynolds in Cwrtmawr, Llanybri. When I am digging or weeding or putting plants in the garden or greenhouse, I can hear the bleating of John Evans, Park Villa's sheep in the field behind me, and I remember that long ago I used to hear the sounds of the cows and other animals from Plasgwyn, next door but one. I used to fetch milk in a can from Plasgwyn, fresh from the cow. I also fetched milk from Arfryn, a farm not far away, up Old Road. Across the road was Ffynnon Fair, whose chickens clucked like background music. These farms are private houses now.

I learned to cook from my mother, but I don't bake bread as she used to. A sunny spot on the wall between our garden and that of Vale View (still known to villagers by its old name, Bull House) next door was the best spot she found for the dough to rise. We did most of our shopping in the village when I was small. Rationing was still on, for one thing. There were several shops in the village. The Stores was the biggest, run by Harry and Mary Jones; Mr Bevan was in the Pound; Griff Jones had a little shop where Ger-yr-Eglwys is now (he ran the Castle Inn as well); Cissie Lewis's sweet shop was in Bristol House; Eireen and Gerald Jones combined the post office with a general store; Ocky Owen the barber had a shop which sold all sorts of things, from postcards to paraffin. We used to buy cakes from Mrs Edwards, Red Lion, when she kept a café there.

For some things we had to go to Carmarthen. The market was a *must* and the buses were packed on market days. My father liked looking round the sale-rooms, especially St Mary's. He bought some nice pieces of furniture there, including a huge, gentleman's wardrobe, which I still have. He got it cheaply at a time when large pieces of furniture were going out of fashion, but he was more concerned with quality craftsmanship than fashion.

I keep up the family tradition of having pets. I have two poodles and a cat. The poodles are getting on in years, but they have had a new lease of life since Pickles, a kitten, joined them. My father was particularly fond of dogs and would make a fuss of them (as I do). Once I got a toy poodle, a bitch, who was no longer needed for breeding. We were horrified to notice when Dad was taking off the big leather belt he wore for work that she cringed and cowered. Obviously, at some time she had been beaten with a belt. At least she didn't have to fear anything like that ever again.

A few years after my father's death, we had another tragedy in the family. My brother Peter, who had Multiple Sclerosis, died in his early forties. The man I married also had Multiple Sclerosis. It was when working in Coombe Cheshire Home that I met my husband, John. I sometimes wonder whether I ended up working in Coombe because there were nurses around the house all through my childhood. Our house was quite big and the District Nurse lodged with us. She had a large district to cover, Llangain, Llangynog, Llanybri and Llansteffan. She had to walk to most of her cases, because petrol was rationed and she was only allowed a car once a month. Local cars did turns taking her out. My mother often went with her for company on her long, lonely travels.

By the time I was married, my mother's health had deteriorated and so I looked after her and John at home. It wasn't always easy, but John's marvellous sense of humour jollied me along. My mother's example as a housewife paid off too and I did have the benefit of modern appliances. It still puzzles me that in spite of all the cooking, baking, cleaning, washing and ironing my mother used to do, she found time to take us for picnics to Scotts' Bay on warm summer days. We would be there all day, until it was time to go home to get food ready for my father.

They are all gone now, John, my parents, my brother and sister. Joan died of cancer a few years ago, in her early sixties. She lived in America. She was always trying to get me to go out and visit, but I am not as adventurous as my mother, who visited Joan twice – and loved it. I miss them all, but I have happy memories and when I am doing things in church, in the garden or in the house. I think of what I owe them and hope that I am doing justice to what they taught me.

Margaret Griffiths.

The last apprentice

Rushing home from Llangathen school and after gulping down some rabbit pie, and Mam's home made blackberry tart, I would dash across the road to the sawmill as we called it.

But its correct title was John Rees & Sons, Steam Sawmills, Coach Builders & Tool Handle Makers, Broad Oak, Carmarthen. It was sited at the rear of Preseli where David Jones now resides. I was entranced with the place and spent as much time as I could there helping out with minor tasks. I became quite useful even though I was still at primary school.

Later, during the latter half of the war I was at Llandeilo Grammar school and itching to leave. I didn't like school much and to father's great dismay and disapproval I left in 1944 and went to work under William Reese at the mill as an apprentice. Established in the latter half of the nineteenth century with the advent of steam power it was a very advanced modern works indeed for its day, almost a hundred years before electricity arrived at Broad Oak in 1950.

To most boys who are fond of wood and mechanical things the scene inside was captivating. The scent of fresh sawn logs, various shaped boards stacked neatly for later assembly into barrows, tool handles etc. Heaps galore of saw dust and the clatter of the belting transmitting power to the machines was a wonder to behold. But the crowning glory of all was the mighty steam engine with its jet black 8ft diameter flywheel and powerful piston gliding forwards and backwards in its bath of oil.

We had a travelling saw bench for converting the tree trunks into boards and planks. This had a circular blade of at least 4ft diameter, but even this size was not enough for the larger trunks. For these it was necessary to upend the trunk and saw it top to bottom by hand with out 7 ft 6 in 'American' crosscut. This would often take a day and half, sometimes more, but time didn't matter so much then.

We also had two other quite heavy benches for various sawing jobs, a very large bandsaw for cutting the curving shape of cart shafts and wheel kerbs, a rounding machine for the rake and brush handles and dowels, a lathe for turning the hubs of wheels and a boring machine. Also there was a smaller bandsaw turned by human muscle (usually mine!)

The men who were employed there between the wars and up to its end were William Reese, the boss, Llewellyn Rees, his nephew and David and John Henri Williams, two brothers from a family of ten boys. They were men to emulate, all non-swearing, non-smoking and teetotal, except Llew who enjoyed a few bottles of Guinness on Saturdays.

Llew had style. He was a smart dresser, a good cricketer and an accomplished ballroom dancer at the Civic Hall dances. He always polished his sparkling brown shoes at 5 p.m. before boarding the David Jones & Sons bus to Bridge Street, Llandeilo, where he lived.

John Henri had left the mill before my time there, and rounded the locality for an insurance company. He was a gentle, sedate type of man, which left him open to silly disparaging remarks by some. Little did they know that John Henri as a machine gunner had endured the mud and blood of Ypres and Passchendaele, ending up wounded in a Bristol hospital. But he survived and lived to be ninety-three.

David was the strong man of the team. He would be up at the crack of the dawn to light the boiler fire to get up steam by about 8 a.m. for some heavy sawing. Fortunately for him, this occurred only every three to four weeks.

It was he who harnessed Bess, our work horse, into the gambo and loaded it with the latest batch of about twenty-four barrows plus rakes, shovel, handles etc., all neatly addressed with brown labels to such distant places as Cwmllynfell, Bridgend, and Llantwit Major.

Crossing the River Towy he would offload his cargo onto the platform of Golden Grove station where they would be picked up by the next goofs train to Carmarthen and then onwards.

We made three types of garden barrow – Farmers, Garden and a shallow-sided model for the coal-mines. The price of a garden barrow, made of Elm, preferably Red Elm with Ash legs and handles, was thirty shillings. Although I could easily assemble two barrows by day, my first pay was only five shillings a week, but it soon rose to seven shillings and six pence, at which point it was suggested that I buy myself a new plane.

This I did from D.P. Davies' Ironmongers (now Peppercorn). It was a Stanley and cost me seven shillings and six pence – a week's wages.

William Rees was a very religious man who walked to chapel at Llangethen three times on Sunday and regularly read his bible in the evening. He was a staunch Liberal and hanging on the wall in his house was a huge photograph of Lloyd George in the full regalia as Chancellor of the Exchequer. He was quite a strict as an employer, but in a kindly way. John Henri said that he wrote to him every day when he was in France.

He must have been sentimental too, because when Bess, our horse, was found dead one morning we never saw him for three days, least of all when the knacker's lorry came to take her away.

One day I was interested to see an old motor bike, rusty and unused, stuffed under the stairs leading to the upper floor. I remember it had no chain but a belt-driven with a Carbide headlamp.

Years later, I discovered that William Reese used to travel to the Glamorganshire valleys collecting orders on this bike.

Sometimes, sadly, we had to make the coffin for the local deceased. The sides came from a timber merchant in Garnant because we did not possess a machine to cut the mouldings to decorate the panels.

But we did make the bottoms and the lids.

There was a stock of such at the far end of the upper floor. When the need arose, with David at one end and me at the other, we would search down the pile selecting a nice one for the lid and one good enough for the bottom. For some reason beyond me at the time we never reached the very bottom until one day William Rees was called by his Maker. We went to the stack boards and tumbled it all to one side, revealing at the bottom a pair of sides strapped together, the beauty of which I had never seen before, nor since. They were Welsh Brown Oak with handsome grain running lengthways and stunning gold flecks rippling across the width.

He had stored them for years for himself or maybe for his wife Letitia if she died before him. William died aged seventy-two.

Letitia was a lovely lady. She gave apples and sweets from the tin box on the mantel-shelf to all the village kids when they ran errands for her. My most vivid memory of her was when she would trudge up the wooden stairway heaving a large cast iron kettle full of boiling water to be poured over the wood as we bent it in to shape. She would then return late tea-time to collect the empty kettle. Commenting on the finished coffin, she would often say '*Na bert*', meaning 'There's pretty.' Leititia died aged ninety-six.

My father was the village tailor, so with Tom Griffiths, the village blacksmith, we were well served with craftsmen. Even though I said that my father was a top-notch tailor, he was regarded in the area around as the best breeches and jodhpur maker.

Blacksmith Tom was a crusty old character and shrewd. He always arranged for the cartwheels to be branded on a Saturday as there was no water supply in the village except one tap on Broad Oak farm well. That's where the kids came in. They were enlisted to carry the large amount of water needed for the banding. The banding process was dramatic and excited the kids tremendously. There were two bellows to the smithy hearth manned by Oliver, Tom's stepson, and the stronger kids, while Tom turned the metal round and round through the white hot fire.

Suddenly Tom decided that the iron bands were ready and the kids would run out to the waiting wheel with their watering cans or tins. The smithy doors would be flung wide open. Oliver and Tom would rush out with one band glowing red gasped between them with heavy tongs and place it one the wooden wheel. The kids would then march around the wheel cooling it with spouts of water as directed by Tom. With shouts of 'less water!' or 'more water!', he prevented the wood from being burnt, but allowed the gaps between the kerbs to close tightly.

Tom had his genial side too. He would give us five shillings, sometimes more, to spend at Llandeilo's June Fair, but we had to do some weeding in his garden first. He also made hoops and hocks for the boys to run to school with. Mine had an extra decorative scroll on the end as a reward for being the best striker (his words not mine).

Andrew Falconer of Berllan Dywyll had modern ideas, one of which was put in effect by William Rees. This was a giant rake about 11ft wide with ash prongs fitted to the front of an old Austin 16 motor car. During haymaking, he would push the hay from the large fields in front of the school and the church in a matter of a few hours. He used knotted ropes tied around the wheels to improve the grip with the help of some human ballast in the back seat. Someone was also needed to guide him through the gateway as he couldn't see a thing owing to the mass of hay in front of him.

When thankfully the war came to an end, life changed dramatically. Pneumatic wheels appeared on our tyres. Superfluous rubber wheels and axles which had once circled the skies of Europe under Spitfires and Hurricanes now transversed Llangathen fields under long trailers pulled by little grey Ferguson tractors.

About this time I was taken ill with a serious illness and did not lift my Stanley plane for four years, by which time the mill was near closure, superseded by electrical and mass production.

But as the years roll by, I feel a great pride and satisfaction to have worked in the age of steam. Thanks to the Almighty I am still here at a time when man can power himself to reach the moon and beyond.

Don Smith

A taste of the good life

We could not have wished for better weather. It was August 1969. My husband and I and our three young children were in South Wales on a two-week camping holiday. We had planned our journey from the Wirral carefully. We were en route to Manorbier but our *Tourist Guide to South Wales* had tempted us to visit Carmarthen Market on our way through. We camped at Abergavenny on Tuesday evening so that we could break camp and arrive in Carmarthen mid-morning on Wednesday.

Carmarthen Market was like no other I had seen. It was vibrant, colourful and alive with the Welsh language. Trestle tables groaned under the weight of the produce for sale. Stepping outside the huge green painted doors at the rear of the market hall we found ourselves in a narrow straw-strewn street. The smell and cries of cattle excited me as well as the children. Hanging onto each other, fearful of being separated or inadvertently obstructing trailers and livestock, we negotiated our way across the street and into the Mart. Farmers young and old, some with sticks, some with pipes or cigarettes hanging from their mouths and most wearing caps or jaunty trilbys, joked and bantered with each other. The auctioneer rattled up the prices so speedily that my un-tuned ears couldn't tell if he was speaking in Welsh or English.

Absorbed with the rhythm of the auction I hadn't been paying attention to the children. A moment of panic, where was five-year-old Gillian?, and then relief at sighting her bright yellow shorts as she peered intently at a pen full of calves. She had spotted a tiny mournful Jersey calf recumbent in the centre of the pen, an older calf was urinating all over it. She looked at John and I with eyes that were as appealing as those of the calf. It was difficult to try to explain why we couldn't rescue it and take it home with us, especially as a

Mount Pleasant, Pen y Bont, 1995.

good-natured farmer had, with a twinkle in his eye, offered to put in a bid for us. Gillian's tears had dried well before we reached Manorbier. The calf was forgotten but not the visit to Carmarthen Market. Many years later when, in answer to John Seymour's *Fat of the Land* and Felicity Kendal and Richard Briers' televized *The Good Life*, we decided that we too wanted to experience the joy of living off the land, Carmarthen was our instant choice.

The market was much changed. The clock tower was still there, carefully restored and designed to blend into the new market building. Gone were the green doors and shutters; no doubt many of the stall holders were the same or at least the sons and daughters of traders we'd seen previously, but the livestock market was no longer in earshot. It had been reconstructed at a more hygienic and vehicle friendly distance. Concrete and steel bars held animals securely – most of the time! But not all of the time as the headlines in *The Carmarthen Journal* on such occasions dramatically pointed out. Straw was not much in evidence and tourists were made to feel ill at ease in this more intensely competitive and businesslike environment.

We moved to Mountpleasant, Pen y Bont, in December 1981, taking over not only the smallholding but also the resident Jersey cow and an assortment of chickens. We brought with us from our half-acre miniholding in the Wirral; six milking goats, six female kids, three geese, three hives of bees and far too much accumulated junk. What we were short of was money to do the essential repairs and renovations to the cottage, and capital to set up a goat farm. It took nearly three years with me working two hundred miles away before our business could finally be launched. We took advice. The man from ADAS was enchanted by our house-pig, the inquisitive goats, Daphne the Jersey, and impressed by our productive vegetable plot. He lingered in the sunshine, enjoying the ambience but then shook his head sadly. 'Well!' he said, 'you have a lovely place here but I don't know how you'll ever make a living from it.'

A few days later an advisor from the Soil Association arrived. He walked every inch of our smallholding. He exclaimed excitedly at the piece of ancient woodland, the pasture containing pignut and anthills, the caterpillar of the drinker moth that he almost stepped on and our sturdy organically grown vegetables. 'Such a beautiful spot. What potential,' he muttered encouragingly. Over lunch, which consisted of a medley of salad vegetables from the vegetable plot, bread from the Rayburn, butter courtesy of Daphne and a choice of my home-made goats' milk soft cheeses; he listened carefully to our plans. He made notes so that he could write back to us with advice on how we should proceed and what options we could usefully consider.

We worked so hard. We had already experienced the heaviest snowfalls in living memory, the 1982 heat-wave, and the wettest autumn on record. We never 'costed' the hours that we put in, for not only were we establishing a cheese making business, we were entering into the whole ethos of an organic lifestyle. It was a hobby and a livelihood that revolved around being as self-reliant and environmentally friendly as possible. We kept the goats that provided the manure that grew the vegetables, which we and the goats then ate. We made cheese and yoghurt to sell along with our organically grown vegetables to a whole food distributor. We sold our surplus eggs to Gwyneth Williams, the proprietor of Pen y Bont village shop. Sadly Gwyneth died in the late 1990s. Now Pen y Bont no longer has a village shop. Weaners purchased from local smallholders were fattened up for the freezer. We utilized whey from the cheese making to soak the barley we bought from a local farm.

It would have been absurd to expect to produce everything on the smallholding but we recycled everything we could. Large empty containers were converted to animal feed troughs. Baling string was used in numerous ways and even things like the strings off cereal bags were carefully conserved for other uses. The woodland generated fallen wood to help fuel the Rayburn, provided blackberries for jam and provided us with a wild area to explore and enjoy in rare time off. We had a large mortgage to pay. This meant that I was single-handed most of the time. Including travelling to and from Carmarthen, John was away from Mountpleasant ten hours per day, five days per week and the children, now adult, only made the journey to Mountpleasant for special events.

The cheese was popular. I progressed to making hard cheese and soon we needed to construct new cheese rooms and a more efficient milking parlour in order to cope with the demand. John Savage of Teify Cheese, Llanddysul, extended retail sales of his cheese from the farm gate to a stall in Carmarthen Market. His objective was to include a range of local and speciality cheeses. I was delighted to see my Pen y Bont goats' cheese displayed for sale on his stall. I had become part of the burgeoning new specialist Welsh Food Industry.

In those early years dairy hygiene regulations were less comprehensive than they are now. The onus for producing safe food lay in the integrity and commitment of the producers. Many small-scale cheese makers delivered their cheeses carefully wrapped and packed into cool boxes in the backs of Land Rovers, or boots of cars. To make deliveries more cost effective producers often swapped and delivered each other's cheeses. It was a common interest in delivering to a London

Pen y Bont goats.

dairy that I came to make friends with Eiddwen Morgan of Nantybwla Cheese. By the time the need for refrigeration was an issue Theo Bond and Richard Harries had stepped into the breach and established Caws Cymru as the leading distributor of Welsh produce.

Eiddwen Morgan and I remained friends. I have spent many happy hours in her company, memorably those spent wandering around the Museum of Welsh Life she has created in one of Nantybwla Farm's redundant buildings. The range of artefacts exhibited cover most aspects of rural Welsh life in the past two hundred years. The collection includes family chattels and heirlooms from both Eiddwen and husband Edward's families. Pointing these out prompts Eiddwen to recount in meticulous, and often amusing, detail events that she remembers, either first hand or as oft told tales from her childhood. The recipe she uses for Nantybwla cheese was handed down from her great-grandmother. In those far off days there was no refrigeration, only larders or dairies on north walls. Every Saturday, Eiddwen's great-grandmother brought her cheese all the way from Llandovery to sell it in Carmarthen Market. She drove herself to Carmarthen on a cart pulled by a Welsh cob.

The introduction of The Farmers Market held on the first Friday of each month in the

Eiddwen Morgan selling Nantybwla cheese, Carmarthen Farmer's Market

Mount Pleasant, Pen y Bont, 1995.

Carmarthen Market precinct means that Eiddwen is also able to follow family tradition and take her cheese from the farm to sell direct to consumers. Browsing among the stalls at The Farmers Market I cannot help feeling a little cheated that this dimension of the market was not available when I was still making cheese. I look at Eiddwen's colourful display of Nantybwla cheeses and remember the times before arthritis took control of most of my joints, when I too was able to make cheese that won prizes at shows and when I also was part of the exciting 'Food from Wales' initiative.

I am no longer physically capable of being a full-time smallholder but at least I was fortunate enough to enjoy many of my small-holding years free from the European intervention that now stifles the small producer. Legislation has since arrived that ignores the wishes of many small farmers and smallholders. No longer is it possible to recycle egg boxes or to have the animals you

Carmarthen Farmer's Market

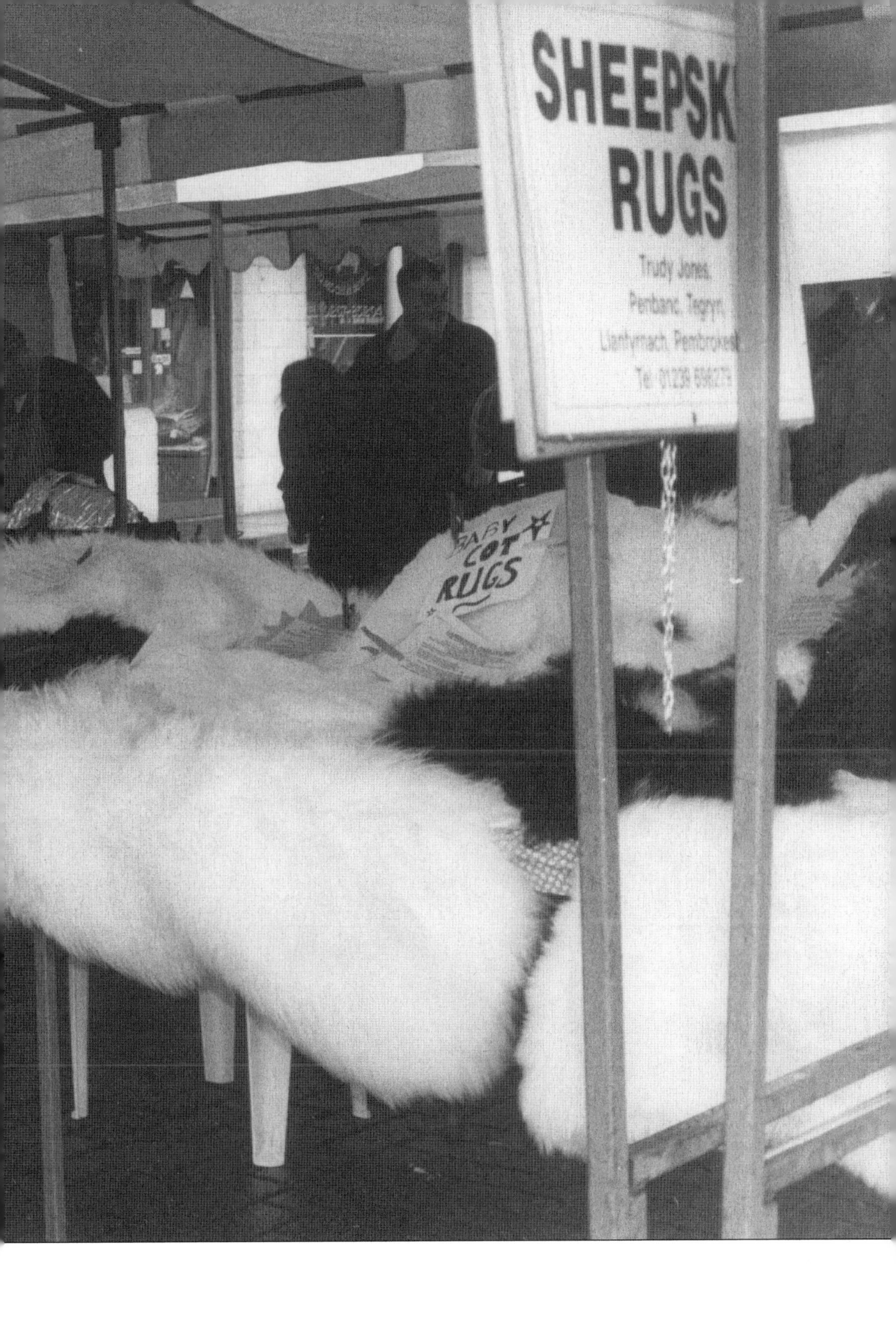
SHEEPSK
RUGS
Trudy Jones,
Penbanc, Tegryn,
BABY
COT
RUGS

have lovingly reared slaughtered in a small and friendly abattoir, like the much-lamented one at St Clears.

Progress will always create winners and losers. Movement of the Mart from Carmarthen town centre has no doubt been a great relief to residents who lived in close proximity. No one wants to run the risk of a terrified bull thundering into their back garden. The town has lost some of its character. Whatever is built on that empty site can never replace the noisy chaos that was the mart. These days tourists do not need livestock markets to acquaint their children with farmyard animals. Progress has encouraged some family farms to diversify and open their gates to welcome tourists with their children into the more appropriate environment of the farm-park. Here calves never have to suffer the indignity of being urinated on by their companions and woolly lambs look far removed from roast dinners.

Jenny White

3 An Introduction to the Town

A walk along Priory Street in 1901

Our guides for this trip along Priory Street in 1901 will be the census and *Kelly's Directory of Monmouthshire and South Wales* for that year. The previous year, according to Lodwick's *The Story of Carmarthen* had seen the tin works close down. As will be seen, many still gave their occupation as tin workers. In 1902, though, the works were dismantled. It was an end of an era, just as a new century began.

The census and the trade directory do not always match up, but that's to be expected when working with more than one source even when they are covering the same street in the same year. We start with our backs to the venerable Saint Peter's church, and will be walking along the right hand side first, then returning to the parish church along the left-hand side.

Space does not permit us to stop at each dwelling along the way, and I've intentionally avoided turning this survey into a list of statistics. So we'll be visiting some of the most typical, and atypical, houses, with a few general comments about the street included to give some idea of the context and to indicate some of the street's features. Now, lets step back to 1901, and take a walk along what has been described as 'probably the oldest street in Carmarthen.'

In the census returns the head of No.1 Priory Street is a widow Anna Davies, but in *Kelly's* under the list of commercial properties her first name becomes Elizabeth. Perhaps some family historians could shed some light on this particular Priory Street mystery. Mrs Davies has five boarders with her on census night, 31 March 1901. She is forty-four and a monoglot Welsh speaker. Consequently, her daughter and son, both polyglots, would have been invaluable in communicating between the landlady and the three English monoglot boarders, one from Staffordshire and two from Herefordshire, who were there at the time.

The Red Lion is next door. It is run by the Tregaron born John Rowlands. Next along is the butcher David Thomas who lived with his sister, a domestic. At No. 4 there is the grocer and coachman, John Griffiths, although in the trade directory he is listed simply as a 'householder'. His wife, Mary, and the fifteen-year-old boarder are both natives of Cardiganshire.

The Old King George, whose seventy-two-year-old innkeeper gave his occupation as 'Licensed victualler', provides the second watering hole on this side of the street. A third is just next to it. Here the head is sixty-year-old Ann Edwards and she bestows upon herself the occupation 'publican' rather than the grander title of her neighbour. In *Kelly's* her premises is described as a 'spirit store'.

Another boarding house at No. 7 includes among its occupants a thirty-year-old boarder David Allan, a Church of England curate. Next door but one is the entrance to Maes-y-Crugiau

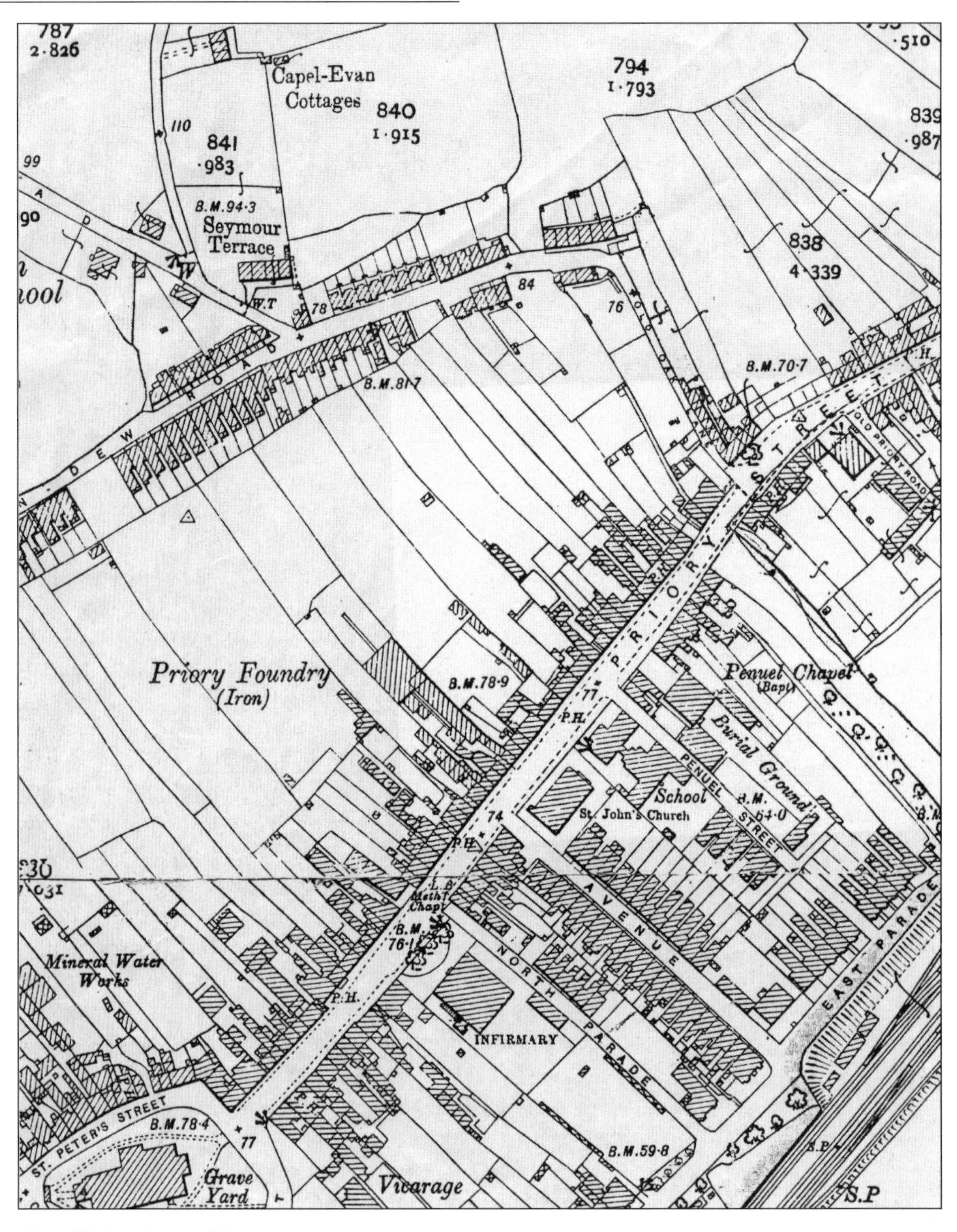

Map of Priory Street, 1901.

Yard. The six properties here are small, mainly two roomed, one of which is shared by a railway carter, his wife and seven children. The nearby Carmarthen Infirmary houses a twenty five-year-old house surgeon, the matron, six nurses, a cook, a housemaid, a ward maid, a laundress and twenty patients. A green grocer's is next to the infirmary. At No. 12, according to the census, there lives a drayman. And another widow, Letitia Davies aged sixty-two, shares her house with her daughter, grandson and three boarders. Two further rooms are occupied by a Neath born sanitary inspector.

There is the same mix of boarders and a two-room lodger next door with Thomas Daniels the tailor. Two of the four boarders are art students who were probably some of the 180 students at the School of Art which had moved from Parade road to Church Lane ten years ago in 1891. The next three houses are occupied by workers employed at the iron and brass foundry. The first by a labourer, the second by a fitter and the third by a smith. Moving along to No. 20, the eighteen-year-old boarder is a dressmaker, an occupation that often appears alongside the names of the young females of the street.

At No. 23, there is a sixty-two-year-old mason and his blind wife, aged seventy. One more along, there's the forty-four-year-old bachelor who works as a roller man at the tinworks. And three sisters, all dressmakers and single, live next door. The sixty-six-year-old tinplate worker and his three sons, one a tinplate worker, another a iron moulder at the foundry, and the eldest a tailor, who lived at No. 27 can quench their thirst at the Cart and Horse. This establishment is run by seventy-two-year-old man with a thirty-five-year-old wife. Perhaps this early twentieth-century sugar daddy drew in the custom of the other tin workers who occupied a number of the houses further along the street. Then again, given the tin plate works closure his customers might be declining. Other occupations present in this part include an accountant, J. Williams at No. 36 and a railway engine driver at No.38. Next door to the engine driver lives Mary James, a fifty-six-year-old widowed butcher. Her son Daniel is a butcher too, but the daughter Elizabeth has opted for teaching.

In the houses from Nos 40 to 49 tin plate workers and their families dominate, though there is also the occasional representative of rail workers, a brakeman at No. 43 and a sixteen-year-old telegraph messenger at No. 42. It is interesting to note that a number of tinplate workers daughters were dressmakers. The head blacksmith at the tin works, William Owen, who'd been born in Glamorganshire, lives at No. 50. This is a four-room house, like the majority in the 40-50 range; though some of them have only three rooms. Number 56 is occupied by David Reed, a rope maker. The following house is occupied by another David, David Davies, a 'shed labourer' working for the Great Western Railway.

Some of the dwellings in Parcel Terrace off Priory Street are very small. 8a has only one room, occupied by the widower Joseph Bowen, a fifty-three-year-old labourer. And two women in their mid-twenties employed at the tin works share two rooms at 8b. Priory Street's second female butcher lives at No. 60. Mary Jones, who unlike Mary James at No. 39 has no son working with her, is seventy-two years old. Another dressmaker lives in the two room dwelling along. She is a young widow of twenty-six years with two young daughters.

The Rope Makers Arms run by George P. Rees, who combines rope making with publican duties, brings us near the end of this side of Priory Street, whose remaining buildings are occupied mainly by tin workers and those employed on the railway. Before turning to the other side of the street, some mention should be made of the carrier service which Priory Street, along with Lammas Street, offers on a Saturday and Wednesday. The compilers of *Kelly's Directory* caution visitors to book a place on these wagons offering to carry people and parcels to nearby villages at the Red Lion, Priory Street, because 'they are not regular in their attendance, nor are there stated times for departure.'

Our journey continues on foot, but we have a new guide, because this side of the street from Nos 65 to 145 was enumerated by Walter Oriel Morgan, whereas the numbers from 1 to 65 were enumerated by David Peter. At No. 66a there is another widow businesswoman, Mary Thomas, a grocer, who lives with her thirty-two-year-old son, a tinplate worker. Next door but one at No. 68 there's an interesting study in language use. Lewis Thomas a tinplate worker is bilingual, while his wife only speaks Welsh. Their seven daughters, the eldest of whom is a dressmaker, are all bilingual, except for the three youngest who are Welsh monoglots like their mother.

In No. 74 the son of the tinplate worker is a county court bailiff. At No. 76 we came across another first in Priory Street, where Thomas Richards, grain merchant and grocer has two servants. In contrast, living in two rooms at 78a are a sixty-year-old general labourer, a widower, and his seven-year-old grandson. Nos 82 to 84 contain twenty-three people from three families. This differs with the four rooms of No. 85 just occupied by David Jones, a railway signalman. At 87a there is another solitary male, the sixty-nine-year-old shoemaker, Abraham Jones, born at Llandefeilog but now living in a single room.

Margaret Peter, the head of the Mason's Arms at No. 88, is unmarried and lives with

Priory Street, 1901.

her niece. In Kelly's she is described as a beer retailer, but her own job definition is the rather more respectable sounding 'licensed victualler'. Next door the tin worker's son has a white-collar job as a solicitor's clerk. His fifteen-year-old sister is another of Priory Street's many dressmakers. Another widow shop owner lives at No. 90 and her three daughters represent a wide range of careers. The eldest, aged twenty-four, is a dressmaker, the middle daughter is an assistant schoolmistress and the youngest, at sixteen, is a 'telegraphist'. More railway workers live at No. 92, where the head of household's son is a railway porter, and at 94 the home of a sixty-one-year-old railway engine driver.

After passing the opening to Oak Yard, where there are two dwellings, we come to

No. 96, or 94 according to *Kelly*'s. The head, David Bassett who was born at Llanelly, is a shoemaker, who also has two boarders at his house, one a lay preacher, the other a shop assistant. At No. 97 there lives Robert Jones, who puts 'manager of the tinplate works' as his occupation. He, like Bassett next door, was born in Llanelly. He has an English wife and of their three children, the younger two only speak English, but the oldest, an eleven-year-old, is bilingual. A Llandeilo born servant also lives at this address.

William C. Taylor, a fifty-eight-year-old railway passenger guard, born in Gloucestershire, lives at No. 102. He is an English monoglot, and given the contact with the public involved in his work one wonders if he ever came across Welsh monoglots. Having said that, the majority of those in Priory Street were bilingual, so perhaps any misunderstandings would be dealt with by bilingual passengers.

A widow with two sons and two male servants occupy the King's Arms at No. 103. At 104a there lives Thomas Rees, a cabinet maker who, widowed, lives with his two sons, aged thirteen and eight, in a one room dwelling. Meanwhile, next door North and South Wales meet, Mary Evans lets out two rooms each to a couple of bank clerks, one born in Cardiff, the other Caernarvonshire.

After 108 Priory Street there is Duke Yard where which consists of seven numbered properties of various sizes, from one room to four and over. In No. 7 lives Priory Street's oldest inhabitant, David Samuel aged ninety, a retired weaver. Living with him are his sixty-year-old son, who is a flannel weaver, and fifty-four-year-old daughter, both single. There's another butchers at No. 110. However, this one is run by a sixty-four-year-old married man and not a widow. Number 111 contains, in addition to the head Mary Evans, three female boarders. Next door is the White Horse, which for some reason was not included in *Kelly's*. The head, Samuel Evans, is a fisherman as well as a publican.

The sixty-year-old china dealer who lives at No. 113 seems to have brought up his son William according to the precepts of the Victorian age because he is now a prison warder. The next three houses are occupied by tin and ironworkers, one of whom is an eighty-six year-old widower. This house, No. 116, stands out for another reason; the active octogenarian's son, Benjamin Jones, is the foundry manager.

Passing No. 119, another business, this time a grocer and flour merchant run by a widow, we arrive at No. 120, where the head of household is Francis Davies, an accountant born at Newcastle Emlyn. If he, or his wife and two children, liked sweets, they were ideally situated because Sarah Bowen ran a confectionary business next door. And you will be surprised, or not as the case may be, to be told that Sarah is a widow.

The timber sawyer at No. 122 has another of the street's pubs next door. The publican of the New King George, Thomas Evans, is a year younger than his wife who is sixty. In fact, many wives are older than their husbands around here. A Calvinistic Methodist minister,

Edward Davies, is a somewhat surprising neighbour. He lives with his five children and is a widower.

A solicitor's clerk, a lady living by her 'own means' and a head police constable, an English monoglot from Swansea, live in the next three houses. The following three are recorded as being 'not in occupation'. David Davies is the innkeeper at the Eagle Inn. He lives with his wife and his thirteen-year-old daughter and Phoebe their servant. On census night they have a visitor, Richard Evans, twenty-three, who is recorded as a 'military man' born in Llandidloes.

A couple, the husband aged fifty-two and the wife fifty-nine, live at No. 132, and a number of tin plate workers and general labourers live in the houses up to No. 138, more commonly known as the Castle Hotel. At 141 we find another engine driver, David Lewis. Next door but one is George Treherne's grocery store, whose sign we can make out from the photograph dating from before 1909. Mr Treherne is forty-nine and his wife is fifty-three They have three sons, a daughter and two servants.

The penultimate house on this side, No. 144, belongs to Rees G. Price, forty-nine, who put down his occupation as 'medical profession'. His daughter who is in her early twenties is recorded as being a 'medical student'. So it seems that from elderly widows keeping shops to young medical students, Priory Street in 1901 has its fair share of career women.

Mike Benbough-Jackson.

Growing up in Carmarthen 1914 – 1930

Prize-winning entry

Recruiting in 1914

In 1911, when I was three, we moved into No. 50 Parcmaen Street. When the First World War broke out in 1914 I can remember walking up to the barracks in Picton Terrace, attracted by the sound of a military band playing. A recruiting drive was on. Men would join up in the barracks and march proudly through town to Guildhall Square. We boys would march alongside. I was only six years of age and can remember running to keep up.

The author, W.L. Davies, aged seven.

The Vints Theatre, Blue Street

The 'Vints' in Blue Street was a lovely theatre, which also showed films. Every Saturday morning we would pay 2d or for admission, to sit in the front rows. Mr Puddicombe would play the piano to accompany the silent films. If there were galloping horses, or a train, Mr Puddicombe would accelerate his playing to match. If it was a love scene he would change key and play accordingly. Some of the children, for devilment, would throw lumps of orange peel at Mr Puddicombe who, when provoked, would stop playing in the middle of a film and shout out 'who did that now?'. Good repertory companies would visit the Vints, with well-known plays. They were happy days. Children didn't get into the sort of trouble they do today, and if we were mischievous we would have a row from our parents.

Horse versus car

In the days of my childhood transport was mainly by horse. Generally the street was free of traffic and we used to play football up and down the street. We used a tennis ball as a football and called the top end of the street the highlands, and the bottom the lowlands. We

Site of the original Vints Theatre.

Christ Church choir, during the First World War.

would tie string from lampost to lampost to make goals. Once in a while our game would be interrupted by a gambo, or a horse-drawn milk float. The gambo would have a shaft sticking out at the back and we used try to sit on it and have a ride. The first car in Parcmaen Street was owned by Mr T.H. Jenkins, a teacher in the Model sschool. I well remember one day Mr Jenkins intended taking his wife, daughter and other relatives to the seaside for the day. The family all emerged and settled themselves into the motor car, which had to be started with a starting handle. Mr Jenkins tried and tried to start the car, but failed, and in due course the family were obliged to process back into the house.

The day the choir went on strike

During the First World War, many of the members of Christ Church choir were away fighting. One day when I was about eight I was on my way to church when the choirboys were assembled inside the vestry of the church. One of the senior boys called me over and said 'Come on, you're joining the choir – put this cassock and surplus on,' and that was my introduction to the choir. The organist was away fighting in the war, and so the vicar's wife used to play the organ and lead the choir. This particular year the boys were annoyed because no 'social' had been organized for us – the tea and games which had been the annual treat. The older boys decided the choir should go on strike in protest, and this particular Sunday I went down to church as usual, to find the senior choirboys assembled on the opposite of the road. 'We're not going in, we're on strike!' was the cry. The junior boys just had to fall in, and instead of going in to the service we set off up Picton Terrace and walked as far as Pontcarreg Farm. That afternoon we all turned up for Sunday school, and the Reverend Griffith Thomas asked the choir boys to stay behind after class. We were all frightened and shaking, and sure enough had a terrific telling off along the 'I hope you are ashamed of yourselves' lines. When we got home word of our 'strike' had got to our parents, and we all had a further telling off. However, the following Thursday Mrs Griffith Thomas put on a tea party for us at the vicarage – and we felt more guilty than ever. I have often thought since of the unusual nerve displayed by the senior choirboys on that occasion. Never before or since have I heard of a choir going on strike.

Minstrel troupe

With all the young men away fighting, a minstrel troupe was formed and I was roped in to appear as a little girl in a wig of long black curls. We all had our faces coloured with burned cork. First we performed in the Saint David's Memorial Hall in Morfa Lane, and I sang a solo, 'I love daddy, my dear daddy, and I know that he loves me. He's my playmate rain or shine, there ain't another daddy in the world like mine'. I was around nine at the time, and later we entertained the wounded soldiers in the Red Cross Hospital in No. 1 Penlan Road, formerly the old workhouse.

Memorial

In around 1919 a memorial tablet was unveiled in Christ Church commemorating those members who had given their lives for their country during the First World War. The ceremony was performed by Sir Owen Phillips of Coombe (later Lord Kilsant), and so many were present that the aisles were filled with extra chairs brought from the church hall. A few days before, Mr Charles Wilford said to me 'I'd like you to sing a short solo – do you think you'll be alright?' and I sang the solo from the anthem, *The heavens are telling*.

Before the age of the telephone

In 1920 I was in the top class in the Model school one day when the headmaster called me out. Harold Greenwood was being tried in the Guildhall for poisoning his wife, and all the national newspapers were in attendance. (He was saved by the evidence of his daughter, who claimed to have drunk the same wine as her mother). They needed a boy to take telegrams from the reporters up to the general post office in King Street, for despatch to waiting Fleet

Class One, Model Infants school, 1915.

Street editors. I had to wait in the office of Mr John Sears, the solicitor (where Woolworths is now) for the telegrams to be brought out, and then run as fast as I could up to King Street. I was paid so much per day, but it was sufficient reward for me to be excused school.

In tune

Another day in the top class, the Head asked if any boy knew music. I was learning to play the piano and so I volunteered. It turned out that the church organs were being tuned, and the visiting tuner (from Bristol) needed someone to play individual notes at the keyboard while he tuned the pipes etc. at the back of the organ. We went from Christ Church, to the English Congregational church, to St David's church, to the Roman Catholic church and finally to the chapel in St David's Hospital. It was boring work for a boy, just playing one note and waiting for the tuner to call 'right, next' and then playing the next. In Christ Church I launched into a rendition of 'Moonlight and Roses' to break the monotony, and almost deafened the tuner. In St David's one of the patients burst into the chapel, pushed me off the seat and started to play a piece of music. The tuner emerged from the organ shouting 'What the bloody hell is going on there?' It turned out the patient was the hospital organist and resented a stranger appearing to take his place. Attendants came to take the patient away.

The remarkable ticket seller

In the 1920s a cashier with remarkable ability worked in the Capitol Cinema. She was the younger daughter of the tailor who lived next door but one to the Congregational Chapel in Lammas Street. The tailor was a brother to Mr Sam Thomas, the talented music teacher of Academy House in Jackson's Lane. She worked in the ticket box, and the Capitol operated a system of two queues – one for the gallery and one for downstairs. Miss Thomas could sell tickets to both queues with amazing speed, calculating change etc. for both queues at the same time and dealing out tickets with both hands. The queues would be dispatched in no time. The public were fascinated to see her work, and I have certainly never seen anyone else work like that in any cinema or theatre.

A tramp answers back

Tramps would usually go the rounds of the town. A tramp would carry a little tin can and knock on the door with the request 'Could you give me some boiling water?' (in the hope that they would be given something better). There was a story going around at that time that a tramp knocked at a door and asked the owner if she could spare him a piece of bread. She was quite religious and returned with a slice of dry bread, saying 'I'm giving you this for the Lord's sake'. The tramp responded 'Well for Christ's sake put a bit of butter on it'!.

How the Charleston dance arrived in Carmarthen

In 1926, when I was eighteen, I was a member of 'The Comets', an amateur concert party of local boys and girls performing for one week at the Empire Theatre in Blue Street, Carmarthen. Mr Willie Sutcliffe was the producer of the show, and the proceeds went to the English congregational church fund. The boys wore yellow trousers and black jackets and bow ties in the show, and the girls wore yellow dresses. The show ran from Monday to Saturday, with a change of programme on the Thursday evening. I was singing the solo part in

Cast of Journey's End, *1930 Cast from left to right: Iori Jenkins (2nd Lt Hibbert), Frank Davies (German soldier), W.G. Jones (Sgt Magor), Fred Price (Lance Cpl Broughton), W.L. Davies (2nd Lt Raleigh), Rowland Jones (2nd Lt Trotter), Harold Lloyd (Capt. Stanhope), Ritchie Davies (Pte Mason), B.J. Evans (Lt Osborne), G. Evans (the Colonel), D. Jenkins (Capt. Hardy and the producer of the play).*

a rendition of 'On the barn, barn barny shore', with the chorus singing the verses. Having recently seen the Charleston performed by a professional couple in the Patti Pavilion in Swansea, in one rehearsal I started doing the Charleston during one of the choruses. Mr Sutcliffe called out 'That's great, we'll put that in the show'. So on the Monday, Tuesday and Wednesday evenings I performed the Charleston, and it was well received. The programme duly changed on the Thursday evening, but the audience had heard about the performance on the previous evenings and they demanded that the Charleston be performed. Mr Sutcliffe told me I would have to go on again, and so the Charleston was performed all the week. On the Saturday night I was encored six times, until I was ready to drop! The dance caught on in Carmarthen and before long there were Charleston competitions in the Drill Hall. I taught Peggy Gardiner the dance, and we entered the competitions as a couple and won them all.

Journey's end

In 1930 I played Lt Raleigh in a production of *Journey's End*, in the Empire Theatre in Blue Street, under the auspices of the British

Legion. This play, by R.C. Sherrif, depicted the harrowing life in the trenches in the First World War. The production included a very realistic reconstruction of a dugout, which exploded and collapsed in the final scene. We then performed the play in a drama competition in Pontyberem, where we lost by only one point to the famous Garrick players. The play was very dramatic and affecting, with the audience moved to tears. The play took a lot out of us, and afterwards it left us all quite depressed. The Empire Theatre was very fine. There were dressing rooms under the stage, which was spacious. The seating was banked, and there was a balcony.

Roller-skating

Off the Old Station Road there was a rink for roller-skating, which later became a cinema and later still a sorting office. My aunt took me there once to watch, when I was very young. The manager was a Mr Walker; he had a waxed moustache, and wore a jacket and breeches. At a later date, there was also roller-skating in the Capitol Cinema in John Street. Mr Albert Henstock opened the Capitol with a skating rink on the ground floor. Then it was converted into a billiard hall and eventually a cinema.

W.L. Davies

Lingering echoes

In February 1942 my family moved into the Police Station, Llansteffan. I was six years old and I had spent all save the first year of my life in Burry Port. Llanelly had been the 'home town,' busy, industrialized Llanelly, with its cacophony of works' hooters and the constant

Sorting Office, theatre, skating rink, off Station Road.

clatter of trains, trucks and trolley-buses. But from now on, 'Going to town' was to signify a jaunt to Carmarthen. Carmarthen was totally different from Llanelly. Its architecture reflected its long history (though naturally I was unaware of its illustrious past at that stage); its heyday as an industrial town was long since over, as was its primacy as a port, but it had status as a county town and its importance to the farming community it served was unchallenged.

I left Llansteffan in 1954 and returned to live there in 1992. Carmarthen was once again my hometown, though familiar landmarks had disappeared or been modernized almost beyond recognition. At least the memory of those lanes and buildings could be conjured up through photographs and paintings. What could not, and can not, be transmitted are the lost sounds that distinguished the town from all other towns. Sounds are evocative and I strive to catch echoes of those that for me epitomised old Carmarthen, the echoes that linger through the years, sparked by some trivial recollection surfacing when least expected.

From 1947 until 1954 I travelled by a Western Welsh bus to attend the Queen Elizabeth Grammar school for Girls, situated next door to the Queen Elizabeth Grammar school for Boys, Richmond Terrace. From Llansteffan to Llangain the bus would reverberate with the sound of Llansteffan boys fighting Llanybri boys, the Wenglish curses of the former competing with the Welsh oaths of the latter, punctuated by the thumps of flailing limbs and falling satchels. As the bus swung round the corner by Morfa Bach, there would be grunts as limbs were disentangled, followed by a scuffling for seats, and then (comparative!) silence as a teacher boarded the bus at the Pilroath stop.

Countless school buses disgorged their human cargo by the roundabout at Francis Terrace. The noise was deafening. Under the eagle eyes of schoolmistresses and schoolmasters, boys and girls made their way up the communal drive in separate groups, but near enough for whispered assignments to be audible below the shrill cries of nubile adolescents. Footsteps echoed on the concrete floors and steps as we raced into our cloakrooms and thence into assembly, held in the school hall, which doubled as a gymnasium, where reproductions of Raphael and Leonardo da Vinci sat oddly with wall-bars. No talking was allowed while we awaited the headmistress, but the silence was periodically broken by a cough or a sneeze and the rustle of a tunic being lifted in order to get a handkerchief out of the pocket of the regulation navy-blue knickers. In unison we greeted the Head, listened to scriptural readings (read with varying degrees of hesitant nervousness by Sixth Formers), sang a hymn more or less in tune and mentally chanted the headmistress's homily of the day, based on a school rule. We knew all the rules by heart and I can still hear her voice admonishing us that 'Girls must walk to and from school in twos, not more than threes, accompanied by members of their own sex.' A piano played a march for our exit, but there was no steady rhythm of marching feet; we were hopeless at keeping in step. To reach our classrooms, we ran the gauntlets of officious prefects reminding us in strident tones that there was 'no talking in the corridors.'

Whenever I visit the County Record Office, which is now housed in my old school, I hear echoes of the scrape of chairs as we rose to greet a teacher in class, the rattle of desk lids as we rummaged for pens and rulers, and the scratching of pen-nibs when past their prime. From the old Domestic Science room comes the clinking of pots and pans and cutlery and from the Science Laboratory the hiss of the bunsen burner and the shattering of glass as yet another tube bit the dust. A Latin lesson might produce the whirr of a clock flying through the air, thrown by a mistress, whose aim was mercifully poor. Sometimes I was sent out of class for talking or giggling. Outside the door I stood, aware of the faint hum of teachers' voices from nearby classrooms and dreading the unmistakable clip-clop of the Headmistress's sensible shoes.

Much-loved sounds were the bells that signified the end of lessons and the toot of the bun-van, which arrived in the school grounds half way through the morning. Chelsea buns were our sole means of sustenance until we got home, because school dinners were inedible. The school canteens serving the boys' school and ours were glorified huts, where the clatter of plates and the shrill 'ugh's' at the sight of a tureen of soggy cabbage effectively dispelled any residual pangs of hunger.

Our non-lunch over, we would escape to the town, with or without permission. On mart days we meandered through the chattering groups of Welsh-speaking farmers, listening to the intonations of Carmarthenshire, Pembrokeshire and Cardiganshire dialects, occasionally leavened with the archaic colloquialisms of Llangennech (my ancestral village). Approaching the pens, we heard the melancholy lowing of cattle and bleating of sheep, and dominating the ring was the auctioneer's incomprehensible patter. The pubs were open all day on mart days and from the wide-open doorways came occasional peals

Capitol Cinema, John Street, previously a skating rink.

of laughter as happy farmers shared a joke. We watched men spitting and shaking hands firmly to seal a bargain before crossing the threshold to celebrate their transaction.

The hum and bustle of the nearby market were irresistible. Not many vendors hollered their wares, usually it was the cockle and laver-bread sellers; others declined to raise their voices as they unrolled swathes of cloth with a flourish, weighed and stamped pats of butter, chopped meat from hanging carcasses, extolled the virtues of home-produced fruit and vegetables, or amicably haggled over china and bric-à-brac. Coins dropped into waiting basins with a satisfying clink. The more permanent stalls had old-fashioned tills, each with its own 'voice' and idiosyncrasies. Barely audible in the symphony of clang, thump, rustle and tinkle was the heart-beat of the market, the undertone of female voices exchanging the latest news – 'Maggie's eldest is getting married,' 'Have you heard about — ? I always said that boy would be trouble, just like his Uncle Fred!'

On mart days, going home from school was an adventure, because the cattle were driven through the streets, along Richmond Terrace, to their destination, the Old Station. It was like a stampede in a Western film. The thunderous roll of the hooves and the cries of the terrified creatures grew louder and louder, and then suddenly they were upon us, a noisy, heaving mass. The little second formers' clung to the older girls, their screams echoing those of the hapless cattle. We pressed ourselves against the walls, closing our eyes, but unable to close our ears. After what seemed like hours, comparative silence fell and we proceeded on our way, an ominous plop signifying that we had trodden in one of the many cowpats left by the retreating herd.

Another source of lunchtime entertainment was the Assizes. Maybe it was because my father was a policeman that I was particularly enamoured of the pomp and panoply of the Law. The cavalcade of cars carrying the judge and his entourage, escorted by motorcycle out-riders, went past the schools and, familiar though the sight became, it never ceased to reduce us a respectful silence. However, in order to see the best part of the proceedings, which was the Proclamation on the steps of the Guildhall, we had to sneak out of school through the back gate, but it was well worth the risk of punishment. The trumpets would sound, and then the Judge and the High Sheriff in their splendid robes, the bewigged barristers and the police in full dress uniform would solemnly mount the steps. An unforgettable spectacle.

School finished at 3.45p.m. and our bus left at 4.30p.m. Expenditure on morning buns meant that I never had any money for going to a café and so I usually haunted the County Library, then situated in Spilman Street. I loved books and my one ambition was to become a librarian. I looked upon the County Library as an annexe to Paradise and on the staff as a highly privileged species. The 'no-talking' rule was enforced in those days and I actually liked the stillness, which gave the thump of a falling book the resonance of a shout. You could even hear the books of your choice being stamped at the counter.

Entranced by the riches on the shelves, I often lost track of time and had to run for the bus, through Queen's Street, across Nott's Square, to Guildhall Square, Darkgate and finally up Lammas Street to the Llansteffan bus-stop outside the Golden Lion. There was considerable bustle in town, as commuters and shoppers hurried to bus stops on all sides of Lammas Street. Companies such as Western Welsh, South Wales, Eynon's, Blossom Pencader, etc. ran frequent services to all parts of Carmarthenshire and beyond. Well-worn engines coughed into life, belched out fumes through rattling exhausts and trundled through streets that were not as yet cluttered with cars.

Compared with those of modern schoolchildren, our misdemeanours appear very tame, but talking in class, 'forgetting' homework, playing with water pistols or breaking one of the many school rules, were punishable offences. One method of punishment has given me a recurring nightmare (should I belatedly sue the Local Education Authority?). In this nightmare I am running frantically through completely deserted market precincts. The sound of my footsteps echo like claps of thunder, while my heart hammers my heaving chest. I race along Mansel Street, my satchel thumping against my aching side. I reach the corner of Lammas Street and my knees give way. I gasp at the sight of the Llansteffan bus receding in the distance. The nightmare is based on an all too familiar scenario. After being kept in after school for some transgression or other, I would be let out just in time to miss the 4.30 p.m. bus. There was an hour to kill before the next bus, an hour in which to think up some specious excuse for my parents. The first time this happened I had the additional anxiety lest the bus-conductor refused to let me use my Season Ticket on a bus that wasn't a school bus, because I had no money to pay the fare. I can still remember the exchange: 'Why weren't you on the school bus?' I blushed furiously, knowing that fellow-villagers were listening with interest for my reply, and the leather straps of my satchel squeaked as I wrung them in despair. My eyes were lowered and slowly filling with tears and so I didn't see the look of understanding dawn on the face of the experienced conductor, but I heard his whispered 'Kept in?' I nodded. He patted my shoulder sympathetically and moved on with the little machine he carried on his shoulder – a click for punching a ticket and a whirr for issuing a ticket, sounds that have long since vanished.

Going to town on a Saturday was rarely connected with school in my case, for I was no sportsman. My prowess on the sports field was such that I came to an amicable arrangement with the gym mistress; I would turn up for dancing (her main interest) and she would punish my absence from any other lessons with the minimal one hundred lines, which my four friends helped to produce, with much scratching of pens and exasperated mutterings when the ink failed to run. Life became easier with the advent of biros.

But to return to Saturdays. Attending first house at either the Lyric or the Capitol was the norm. There was a school rule that we were not to go to the cinema unless the headmistress approved of the film, in which case we were to attend the matinée performance. Poor Miss Davies! She would not have lived into her nineties had she gone to one of the cinemas on a Saturday evening and seen most of her fifth and sixth formers occupying the back seats, rarely 'accompanied by a member of their own sex.' How many people remember the sounds of queuing to go in? 'Look, there's Joan. She's with Jim!' 'Sheila will be furious.' 'I'll tell Mam you've been in the pictures.' 'Don't you dare, or I'll tell her about you smoking.' 'Oh, I like your new cardigan.' 'It's my sister's. She doesn't know I've borrowed it.' 'I think Frank Sinatra is wonderful.' 'I like Bing Crosby best.' 'How much longer are we going to have to wait? My feet are killing me.' From the commissionaire – 'Room for two on the balcony and three in the front downstairs.'

The usherette's torch guided us to our seats and was invariably withdrawn too soon. 'I'm so sorry,' you muttered, hastily rising from a stranger's lap. Shuffle, shuffle, crash – the seats lower into place. Eventually ensconced in the comfortable semi-darkness, our eyes focussed onto the screen as the familiar signature tune of *Pathé* or *Movietone News* rang out. Trailers, cartoons, the big picture and advertisements brought in their wake a variety of sounds, some of which, like the whoop of arrow-shooting Indians, we knew we would never experience in reality. Around us were other noises: the crackle of sweet-wrappers being unfolded, the swish of clothing being surreptitiously adjusted by daring hands, the slurp of amateurish kissing. During the interval, the spotlight falls on an alluringly-dressed usherette, the embodiment of adolescent fantasies, carrying a tray supported by a strap positioned around her neck. 'Cigarettes!, ice cream!,' she cries and disappears from view as lusty males swarm into her orbit.

The film-show ended around 8 p.m. and my bus left at 9.00. If I was with my girlfriends, I adjourned to the hiss and sizzle of a chip-shop, but when I was 'keeping company,' I followed in the wake of courting couples, down Friars' Lane, past the gas-works, down to the riverside. It was so romantic, holding hands and kissing to the reassuring murmur of the river and the soft whoosh of a pair of ghostly coracles moving slowly with their net across the dark waters.

Thank God for memory and for the echoes from a happy past that linger in its nooks and crannies.

Eiluned Rees.

The story of Queenie One

The Royal Observer Corps was originally formed in the 1920s to be the 'eyes and ears ' of the fledgling Royal Air Force and its members were Special Constables detailed to keep a lookout. These observers were volunteers with no special training who were initially spread out rather thinly along the south coast of the British Isles but, with the rise of the Nazi threat from Germany, the organisation was refined and it was decided to enlist recruits specially for the service. By 1939 the Corps had been put on a proper basis with reporting centres in strategic towns and a network of posts spread out across most of the southern and eastern counties of England. The rudimentary radar stations that had been constructed in great secrecy in Kent were, by the start of the war, only just becoming operational and were never to cover more than a small part of these islands. It was at that time that the need for a twenty-four hour watch was decreed, and the Special Constables and other unpaid volunteers were obviously not going to be able to provide such a service – so from then on, observers were to be paid the princely sum of £3 per week full-time.

The middle of 1940 saw the German armies occupying the coast of France and it was this that precipitated the extension of the service to all the remaining parts of the British Isles, including West Wales. The airfields of Brittany and Normandy were now on our doorstep. The West Wales Area was to have a plotting centre in Carmarthen and a basement of the Lyric buildings (now occupied by a night-club) was selected as being sufficiently deep underground to be safe from the sort of bombs then anticipated. The plotting centre collated reports of aircraft from all the observer posts in West Wales.

The observer posts were to be constructed on various hilltops with Penlan Hill above the town being the nearest. Other hilltop sites approximately ten miles apart were chosen and included, amongst others, Kidwelly and Dryslwyn. The recruitment of observers commenced by canvassing the members of the ARP (Air Raid Precautions) detachments in the town who were, of course, all volunteers. The ones who would be on watch during the daytime were to be full-time and those who had regular jobs would be part-time and be on duty at night.

This was the signal for my father, who had served at Gallipoli in the First World War, to enrol as a full-time observer in charge of the Penlan Post, which was designated Q1. It soon became known however, in the terminology of the day, as Queenie One. As my parents ran

Post Queenie 1 on Penlan Hill, 1940-1941.

their own shop in town, my father's absence during the day did not cause a lot of inconvenience as the lack of stock to sell during the war years meant that the Royal Observer Corps became his main job, with the shop taking a back seat.

The first post was a rudimentary hut set on the boundary of the large field on the top of Penlan Hill overlooking the town. There was a clear view as far as the adjoining Posts already mentioned and in some directions much further. My father then set about recruiting his observers, about thirteen in number, some of whom were ex-servicemen while the others were either over-age or under-age for the armed forces. Women observers were definitely recruited but they all seemed to end up in the centre on the plotting tables. Everyone was given a beret and a voluminous weatherproof coat and the post was equipped with a telephone connected to the centre and a pair of binoculars; that was how Q1 came into being, to be continuously manned for the next four years.

Within the space of a few months the hut was replaced by a grander structure with an observation tower equipped with a type of theodolite, called a ranging instrument, which could plot the position of an aircraft on a squared map of the area beneath, once its height had been estimated. Then, gradually, the post acquired various homely comforts, such as a stove (very necessary in the bitter winter of 1940/41), a chemical toilet, and an assortment of model planes, supplied by the Air Ministry, to aid recognition. Proper RAF blue battle-dress uniforms made an appearance and the equipment supplied included a chest mike and headphones (to allow the observer to use his ranging instrument and report at the same time) and a tin hat and a service rifle with about a dozen rounds of ammunition. The use of this last item was always a mystery – presumably it was for rounding-up parachuting German airmen – but it was occasionally put to use bagging rabbits to augment the seriously depleted meat ration that everyone endured. Great care had to be taken, however, as a misplaced shot with the Service Rifle could easily blow the anticipated supper to smithereens. It was usually much easier to use one of the .22 rifles that several of the Observers owned. Ammunition never seemed to be a problem, whether it was .303 or .22 as, with the Home Guard and regular troops using every available rifle range in the vicinity, there was plenty about and the authorities were positively encouraging everybody to become proficient marksmen.

The dark nights of 1940-41 became busy when German raiders bombing the midlands, north-west and Belfast from their bases in western France were passing over Carmarthen nightly. Of course there was no real means of identifying the aircraft as they passed over, but the slow beat of their engines was quite distinctive. It was unlike that of the RAF aircraft since the Germans had, so it was explained to me, managed to synchronise the engines of twin-engined planes, so producing the slow throbbing beat that announced their presence. The tracks plotted by the observer posts and transmitted to their centres were the only means the Government had in those days of following enemy planes and so having some idea of which city was to get a raid that night. Air-raid warnings could then be given in good time. It has since become apparent that there were very few defences over the western part of the UK and the German aircraft had the night sky to themselves.

The lighter nights of the following summer brought a diminution of enemy

Post Queenie 1 group photograph, 1943.

activity and the increasing war effort in this country meant many more friendly planes on the horizon, all of which were followed with close attention. There are numerous recorded instances of aircraft getting lost and being guided back to their landing grounds after ROC plots gave controllers on the ground some idea of where the errant plane was going!

Originally the Corps was only called upon to report aircraft, but aircraft recognition was soon a necessity to be able to tell friend from foe. The men of Queenie One, like their fellow observers all over the country, were soon engaged in tests and competitions in aircraft recognition. There were books and magazines on the subject, flash card silhouettes of every conceivable aeroplane that had ever flown, and the aircraft models to which I have already referred. The competitions and exams for which observers were entered often resulted in flamboyant certificates and publicity. The authorities were obviously not going to leave any stone unturned in order to galvanise the observers and prevent friendly aircraft being shot at or even shot down.

By the time the USA had entered the war at the end of 1941, German raids in the West Country and Wales had diminished in number to nuisance proportions and, from then on, there were many more friendly planes of all nationalities to be tracked. A diversion to this state of affairs came about in the summer of 1942 when the post at Kidwelly was heard to report a plane in the vicinity. (Groups of posts were connected by telephone in a net of about half a dozen, so that each post could hear what the others were reporting.) The plane, which was actually a German Fokke-Wolf 190, was completely lost and circling the airfield at Pembrey, the pilot apparently having had the mistaken belief that he was over Brittany. The runway lights were switched on, presumably by mistake, the FW190 landed much to the surprise of all concerned, and became a prize capture which was kept under the strictest secrecy. The Luftwaffe was supposed to imagine that its most secret weapon had been lost at sea, instead of being in the hands of our scientists who were eager to get hold of all of its mysteries. The observers who had witnessed the event, or heard the reports on the common intercom, were very good at keeping secrets!

The year 1944 saw a great increase in activity with the US Air Force bombing all over the Continent in daylight. Many of the planes taking part in these raids, especially when they were over France following the invasion, returned to their bases by flying directly over the town. It was a sight to raise the spirits, after so many years of bad news, to see these great armadas of Flying Fortresses passing low over the town.

It was a testimony to the resilience of the observers, many of whom were not in the first flush of youth, that they managed to struggle up the steep path to the post day after day and night after night for over four years. The members who manned Queenie One were virtually unchanged during the whole of the time that it operated. Mind you it was not all long faces and serious talk. One rather eccentric observer was known to carry a large loaded service revolver with him when negotiating the dark and steep path up the hill. This, he assured his colleagues, was to put paid to any German spy who might be lurking in the shadows. (The early years of the war were plagued by rumours and counter-rumours of spies and parachutists.) Some of the observers resolved to play a trick one dark night by pulling a stuffed sack attached to a chain across the path between high hedges as he approached. He naturally drew his weapon and let fly with a volley of shots, putting the pranksters in fear of their lives. I believe he spent the rest of his time in the ROC embroidering this story with as many fantastic embellishments as his various listeners would swallow.

The occupation of France by the Allies meant that enemy aircraft were no longer a threat to this country and, by the end of 1944, the ROC was being wound down. I'm not exactly sure when Queenie One was finally abandoned, but it was probably sometime at the beginning of 1945. The Royal Observer Corps as a national organisation was finally stood down on the 12 May 1945, and the 1,400 observer posts, that had covered the whole of the British Isles, ceased to exist.

My connection with all that I have related was only as a schoolboy witnessing one of the most exciting times of my life. I spent many happy hours at Queenie One and these few notes may serve as a reminder of a facet of the 1939-45 war as it affected Carmarthen.

Victor G. Lodwick.

4 Education

'An ornament to the Principality' – the origins and development of Trinity College, Carmarthen

When Trinity College, or the South Wales and Monmouthshire Training College as it was originally known, opened in 1848 its first intake of twenty-two students embarked on their teacher training during a remarkable period in history. These young men were the first generation to experience photography in its popular form, would soon be the first to experience a railway journey and would have been among the earliest rugby players in Wales. But they also lived through the 'Hungry Forties' that drove thousands of Irish into south and west Wales as they endeavoured to escape the Great Famine. They also witnessed the cholera outbreak in 1849 that claimed 142 victims in the borough of Carmarthen alone. Eight of the first students had fathers who were farmers and so it is likely that they would have had an intimate knowledge of tensions within the agricultural community, as manifested by the Rebecca rioters who attacked tollgates and the Carmarthen workhouse in the early 1840s.

The reasoning behind the opening of the college was largely in response to the poor state of education in Wales. As the college was nearing its completion, the government issued

College opening, 1848.

Students, Trinity College, 1908.

the 1847 report into the state of education in Wales. The report, commonly known as the Blue Books, aroused much hostility on account of its derogatory picture of Welsh life and its dismissal of the Welsh language as a 'great evil' that hindered intellectual and moral advancement. As Hywel Teifi Edwards put it, for one thing the report made out that immorality was the national industry in Wales. However, few contemporaries disagreed with the findings that improvements in education were needed. It was estimated that seventy per cent of children in 1847 were not attending school. Typical of comments on standards in schools were those which said that children did not know the capital of England, were shaky in their mental mathematics, believed that Napoleon was a Scotsman, and struggled to recount the ten commandments. Moreover, at the time of the report only one in eight teachers in the shires of Carmarthen, Pembroke and Glamorgan had received any formal training, the average period of which was only seven months. It was widely believed that education could address many of the moral and social concerns of the day. More schools were needed in which pupils (as future citizens) were taught by trained masters how to behave themselves. The new Carmarthen training college 'on the hill' would lead the way by equipping these schools with a new breed of qualified teachers who could set the right examples. Carmarthen training college, in the words of its first principal, was to be at the forefront of an educational revolution.

The original name of the college reflected the wide ambition of its founders. Elementary schools throughout South Wales and Monmouthshire were to benefit from well-trained teachers, while North Wales was to have its own training college. Carmarthen was chosen partly because of the personal support that could be provided by the bishop of St David's from his nearby residence in Abergwili.

The mission statement of the college was threefold: to train teachers for church schools, promote Welsh culture and instil Christian values in education.

On 16 July 1847, a crowd of 6,000 watched a procession make its way from Carmarthen market up to Job's Well field, the chosen site for the college, where Bishop Connop Thirlwall laid the foundation stone. The college formally opened on 24 October 1848, at a cost of £9000, most of which was derived from Anglican funds. Upon completion the new Gothic-style college was described in the *Carmarthen Journal* as 'an ornament to the Principality.' An important part of the project included the building of a Model school, located off St Catherine's Street. This was to act as a model of good practice in the district. By the early 1900s, students were placed in schools throughout the county.

Most of the early students were local 'respectable' working-class men, who were already earning a living in occupations such as carpenters, shop assistants, clerks and printers. They were all expected to be active churchgoers and be of good moral standing in the community. On a practical level, students were required to bring along a lengthy list of items. These included: six day shirts, four pocket handkerchiefs, three pairs of shoes or boots, two hats or caps, one hair brush, one large and one fine comb, a tooth brush, a box of drawing instruments and a copy of the *Book of Common Prayer.*

In its early years, the college struggled to keep financially afloat in the face of mismanagement of funds, poor recruitment, and a general 'cooling off' from private benefactors. It very nearly closed within a decade of its opening. In the mid-1860s the strained relationships between William Reed, the first principal, and the college governors did not help matters. Reed was finally forced to leave following an inquiry into alleged mixing of personal and college funds. As a

College gates, 1864.

keen gardener, Reed made sure that he uprooted the rhubarb plants and bee-house before he left. The gradual deterioration in staff morale is indicated in the diaries of Vice-Principal William Edmunds, second-in-command. He complained in particular about the third staff member who took a fancy to a lady in Millbrook (Johnstown). As a consequence he frequently arrived back in college late at night, missed lectures, secretly married her in Bristol and then resigned.

In addition to staffing difficulties, the college authorities faced the ongoing problem of securing sufficient intake figures. As a church college, Anglicans were given preference on admission but recruiting young churchmen in strongly Nonconformist communities proved difficult. Out of necessity, the college accepted non-Anglicans and generally relationships among students of all faiths were good. Recruitment problems were compounded by the fact that teaching was not an attractive career in the mid-Victorian period. Pay and working conditions were poor, especially in rural areas where teachers often held down other jobs to supplement their meagre wages. Stress levels increased from the 1860s when salaries were dependent upon successful examination results of pupils in reading, writing, arithmetic and needlework (for girls) - cramming and rote learning became the preferred methods of teaching. Ex-students serving as teachers in the schools of Carmarthenshire at this time noted their everyday concerns in logbooks. David Jenkins, for example, left the college in 1870 to take charge of a small village school and observed: 'I do great efforts to improve the children in the three Rs, hoping to have a favourable result.' Disappointment at the performance meant that Jenkins left the school, which had to close temporarily as the managers sought a replacement.

The extension of the railway to Carmarthen in 1852 made it easier for the college to attract students from further afield. Using the Church network, students from Yorkshire, the Midlands, London, Devon and East Anglia were soon admitted. Pressures on recruitment also eased considerably following the introduction of compulsory elementary schooling from 1870 and the subsequent expansion in educational provision. This required more trained teachers, which brought increased government grants. Under astute management, the college was placed in a

The Training College, 1864.

secure position by the early 1900s. But it still remained a small, intimate place – no more than eighty or so students were admitted at any one time before the First World War.

Everyday life for students remained remarkably unchanged for much of its history through to the 1940's. It revolved around a semi-monastic routine of study, worship and manual labour. The college authorities also recognised the importance of recreation in such a closely-knit, male-only college. Hence a range of clubs and societies were established and reflected the fashions of the day, such as photography in the 1880s, and public debating in the 1920s.

The daily routine began early. Students rose at 5.30 a.m. every morning and attended compulsory physical drill and chapel before breakfast at 8.00 a.m. Students then attended three hours of lectures in the morning and three hours in the afternoon. They were also required to undertake a range of manual chores, such as mucking out the pigsties or gardening, partly to keep them fit and healthy but also to remind them of the importance of humility associated with the office of being a schoolteacher. Domestic chores and study continued until 9.00 p.m. every night. Students were expected to put their lights out by 10p.m. The name given to the early students, 'inmates', reflected the mentality of this rigid regime.

The nineteenth-century college curriculum reflected the dual Church and Classical influence. For much of its history, the college Principal and lecturing staff were Anglicans who had usually moved up from teaching in a grammar or public school. As part of their course work, students read Church history, explored finer points of theology, learned passages of the bible off by heart, and read Euclid. Rugby and cricket were the major mid-Victorian sports and provided rare opportunities for students to mix with locals in arranged matches.

However, contact with the outside world was highly regulated until after the Second World War. There were genuine concerns over the unwholesome, corrupting influences afforded by the plethora of Carmarthen inns. In 1882 a visiting Her Majesty's Inspector pointedly advised the college council that its students should 'shake off the young men of the town as much as possible.' Social and cultural developments, such as the rise of the cinema, often occupied the minds of college managers as they deliberated over the possible negative effects on prospective teachers. Attending the Lyric Theatre was seen to be a dangerous pastime with its portrayal of the seamy side of life. In 1935 the Principal warned students that they should not be watching sentimental and emotionally-charged films because these were values which Christians rejected. In theory, no students were allowed out of the college grounds without express permission from the Principal although college discipline books show a steady stream of offending students over the years. A rigid system of fines operated designed to keep the students in check - in the 1920s, for instance, a 3d fine was to be paid if the students were caught associating with girls in town. During allocated free time, a monitor was appointed to ring a bell to summon all students out walking in the immediate vicinity back to college. The college gates stood as a literal and symbolic divide well into the twentieth century.

During the first half of the twentieth century, there were a number of key developments in the college and its relationship to the town. After 1907, the college admitted non-residential students to comply with government requirements to further open up teacher training to all faiths. Where possible, non-Anglicans were accommodated in town, which provided a useful boost to the local economy, while allowing the college to retain its Anglican ethos. Over the years more and more students from different religious backgrounds were admitted and many actually shared in the services held in the new chapel, built in 1931, after which the college adopted the name 'Trinity'. The fabric of the college changed considerably in line with the expansion in education after the Second World War. New hostels, a resource centre, swimming pool, and a union reflected a growing sense of optimism, so much so that the college finally admitted female students in 1957, albeit rather nervously.

The Second World War was a key watershed in changing social attitudes. Slowly the college responded to the views expressed by students who wanted more freedom and say in college life. This resulted in closer links within the community as when, for instance, the Student Rag became an established event. In a context of the so-called permissive society, students began to voice their protests over a number of internal issues, such as perceived excessive examinations, restrictive hostel regulations and the limited role of the Student Union.

Most notably in the 1960s and 1970s, students successfully campaigned on behalf of the Welsh language movement. Particularly in the post-war years, Welsh-medium culture has steadily flourished and the college has a proud record of achievement at the National and Urdd Eisteddfodau. A vibrant Welsh department, led by the likes of the late Professor Jac L. Williams, Miss Norah Isaac, Carwyn James and others, succeeded in raising the profile of the language and culture both within the college and the wider community. Many on the staff sympathised fully with the concerns of Cymdeithas yr Iaith Gymraeg (the Welsh Language Society) that Welsh was not receiving the official support that it deserved. Several were active in the local drive for a Welsh-medium secondary school, which led

View of Trinity College, 1900.

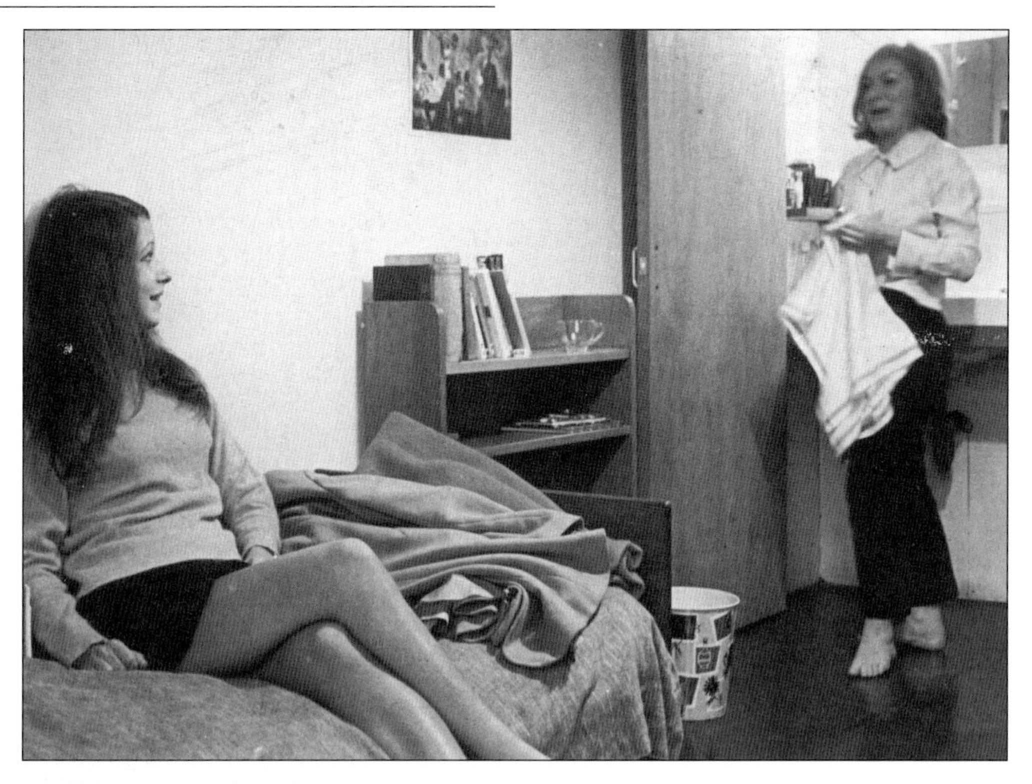

Myrddin Women's Hostel, October 1968.

to the opening of Ysgol Bro Myrddin in 1972. Following the 1988 Education Act, which established Welsh as a statutory subject on the school curriculum, the college has benefited from increased funding initiatives for Welsh-medium courses.

The past twenty-five years have seen a period of continuous change at Trinity, as in all institutions of higher education, with enforced diversification. Responding to the unfavourable economic climate of the mid-1970s and the declining birth rate, which brought cutbacks in teacher training, Trinity successfully offered courses to recruit students other than potential teachers. Since then full-time student numbers have risen from about 500 to over 1,700. In recent years a steady influx of Irish students has added a fresh dimension to student life. Trinity now provides a range of undergraduate and postgraduate degree courses in addition to teacher training. Investment in facilities such as the Halliwell theatre, which opened in 1989, has endeavoured to broaden the appeal of the college.

Undoubtedly, Trinity has acted as an important facilitator in bringing new initiatives to the community, such as the government drive for 'lifelong learning', which has resulted in a range of flexible courses. The shared use of college facilities by local authorities is just one example of mutual support between college and community. Over the years the presence of Trinity has been a major boon to the development of Carmarthen. Successive generations of staff and students have contributed to its social, cultural and economic prosperity. In educational terms, for more than 150 years schools throughout the county and beyond have been, for the most part, equipped with a

The view from Tower Hostel, 1968.

stock of good quality teachers.

In the 1975 annual report for the college, Principal Mansel Jones pointed to the historic need to preserve Trinity's independence as a Church college but at the same time acknowledge the need to move on by working more closely with other colleges. Since then the college has found itself in a similar position in the context of pressure to rationalise higher education in Wales. In the rollercoaster ride of recent changes in higher education it is difficult to keep a handle on the significance of particular decisions. However, it is clear from the past that Trinity has survived because it has adapted when necessary without losing sight of the constants of high quality teacher-training, Welsh culture and a Christian-based education that many still regard as essential contributions to the continued welfare of Carmarthen and society at large.

Russell Grigg.

A Carmarthen art student in the 1950s/60s

I was living on a small farm near Lampeter, and on gaining my 'O' Levels at Lampeter Secondary school it was decided that I should attend Carmarthen School of Art at the age of fifteen in 1958.

The Art school was situated in a former mansion called 'Ucheldir ' at the top of Picton Avenue. (Nowadays it is the Fire Brigade Headquarters). The art students, prior to the early fifties, had always been taught at a college situated in St Peter's Street (now known as the Oriel Gallery).

I met the Principal, Stanley Lewis, ARCA, during an interview in late summer 1958, also Winifred Thomas and John Petts, the staff at the college at the time. Later on I was to develop a long-standing friendship with both Win and John, who were influential in my development as an artist and teacher.

Stanley Lewis was an eccentric man, small and bird-like with a mop of grey hair flying from the base of his bald head. We students used to call him 'Llew', the reason for this I cannot remember, but he certainly prowled his domain with quick authority. He was a good teacher, but inclined to ramble on about 'the war – 'do you follow – do you follow - the war-when I was in the war – in the parachute planes – what was I doing? – drawing – drawing – do you follow? Sketchbooks very important – everywhere – do you follow?' This information was usually punctuated by a long forefinger poking you in the upper part of your arm. Several nights I would go home with a bruised arm due to 'Llew's instruction! The staff, Win Thomas and John Petts, also had the same treatment. It was quite amusing to see them both attempting to put distance between themselves and the principal along the corridors of Ucheldir!

There were only eight students taking the course in my year, and some others who did not stay long and moved to other careers. There were several classes of girls who took 'dressmaking' with Win Thomas, but we did not get to know them very well, as their courses were part-time. Each week we would have two days of life-drawing, taught by Mr Lewis. Each morning Mr Lewis would 'set the pose' with our regular model Margaret, a very pleasant woman who lived in a cottage in Whitland. We would sit at our 'donkeys' (an easel with a seat) and attempt to understand the finer points of anatomy. 'Llew' would move from student to student making elaborate explanatory drawings on our sheets of work, interspersed with the usual tales of 'the war' and 'do you follow?'

Other days were taken up with weaving which I had chosen as my major craft; Win Thomas was my tutor and spent many hours explaining drafting and setting up of four shaft foot looms. She was a very elegant looking woman, with large brown eyes and hair in an 'arty bun.' She became a very good friend to me, many a time she would invite me to her house in St David's Avenue, after college, to talk and have coffee. I was struck by her innate intuition to arrange her possessions within her house so aesthetically – everything was in balance and composed. A true artist's home.

Apart from life drawing and weaving, intermediate students had to complete studies of anatomy, architecture. I remember struggling with a huge volume of *Bannister Fletcher*, making drawings of the 'Ziggurat at Ur!' History of Art was a self-taught affair and, of course, the 'sketch book' and craft book studies' constantly poured over by 'Llew' on a regular basis with very unflattering comments! Our year designed the Carmarthen art school scarf, coloured purple, black and yellow with a pale blue stripe.

John Petts was a person who one was much in awe of as a student; he took us for Basic Design and Lithography and Calligraphy. His understanding of form was unique. He looked so impressive in his white overall coat covered in litho ink, instructing us on how to use the litho press. I still have a small litho print of a horse – the result of an encouraging talk with John. Later on, when I had left Carmarthen and was attending Camberwell School of art for an N.D.D. in Textile Design I was to spend part of the summer holidays at John's workshop in Llansteffan – carrying out simple tasks to help with his stained glass designs. At the time he was working on the Birmingham, Alabama window for Wales after the assassination of Martin Luther King. I still have a very close relationship with Kusha Petts, his wife, an artist of extraordinary talents in many directions. Kusha would come to the Christmas 'Art' parties, at Ucheldir and dance with all the students – these were wonderful occasions for socialising with the other major field students.

Art students outside Ucheldir entrance porch, June 1961.

Ucheldire rear garden terrace, under the cherry tress, 1961.

We all felt very debauched – but looking back the parties were very innocent – there was no hard drug taking in this area in those days.

During the summer term, exams loomed; my friend Audrey, who was from Llandovery, and I, lodged in a small house in Water Street (now a dental practice). Mrs Rees was the elderly owner of the house, a quaint old lady who would feed us on 'lovely boiled onions for your tea – girls.' Being away from home and lodging in Carmarthen for the week was quite an adventure for two country girls. We visited the old market, sadly gone when the market was rebuilt. I remember going to the Plume of Feathers in St Mary Street, being a 'poor art student' I could not afford my favourite vodka and lime! – some farmers in the bar told they would buy me as many vodkas and lime as I wanted if I would drink a pint of beer. I did not resist the offer, and paid dearly for it when I was violently sick in the ladies toilet in the cellar in the pub later!

Every morning of college term, I would arrive at the bus stop near St Peter's church, from Lampeter, and later on from Brechfa (where my parents had moved to at the time). I would walk through the town, down King Street, calling sometimes at Lodwicks Music Store to listen to the latest Elvis music in the booth there, and chat to my friend Sheila, who was an assistant in the shop. Carrying on past Woolworths and Guildhall Square into Dark Gate, there was a butcher's shop across the road (where the craft shop is now) with sawdust on the floor and huge wooden butcher's benches. Sometimes I would call in at Heddon's tobacconist to purchase five Admiral Cigs (I had been accepted into the 'social circle' of art students by stopping at afternoon break for a fag and a chat). Then up Lammas Street and onto Picton terrace, with its elegant pollared trees and Victorian terrace houses.

It was an exciting time in the fifties and early sixties in Carmarthen. As art students we were all

Looking through the balustrades in the Ucheldire garden.

Road to the old Gas Works, 1960.

Lammas Street, 1969.

well known in the town, and often labelled as 'beatniks' – probably due to the fact we would walk into town bare footed on hot summer days dressed in paint spattered clothes, living up to our name! Other students gave me the affectionate name of 'the long black-legged Reely Bird.' I used to wear black tights, leggings, baggy purple jumper and hair in bouffant beehive style!

I eventually managed to pass my intermediate examination and go to London to continue my career. Mr Lewis had lectured me constantly on the opportunities for young people. I remember him telling me once about the 'job' at Trinity College Art Department (which had just been appointed at the time) where a young girl had been given a lectureship without a teaching degree – she could only be an assistant lecturer due to this. 'You could do that job, Awr Awrelia' as he used to call me, 'but you must get qualified.' I did get qualified and eventually I did get 'the job' at Trinity College, where I spent thirty happy years encouraging other students. Now, in retirement, I still have a close relationship with Trinity College as a part-time tutor in teaching practice supervision; the memories of the Art School at Ucheldir and all the fun and experiences of the late fifties and sixties in Carmarthen will never be erased from my memory.

Aurelia Reynolds.

A schoolboy's memories of Carmarthen before and during the Second World War

My schooldays commenced in the Pentrepoeth Infants' school in 1935 and although I must have been taken there by an adult, I now have no recollection of the short walk from our house in Quay Street. In those days the lessons were highly regulated even in the Infants' section with a lot of chanting, singing and everyone sitting in neat rows facing the teacher. I remember quite clearly that during the summer months a canvas awning was erected across part of the tarmac playground so that lessons could be taken in the open air – this was presumably in support of the theory that copious supplies of fresh air was a preventative against various diseases such as tuberculosis. There was no doubt that some of the children lived in unsanitary dwellings, as we witnessed every day in the surrounding neighbourhood.

When I was seven my class was moved next door to the Junior school where we were segregated: boys upstairs with a playground facing Orchard Street and the girls downstairs with the use of the Little Water Street playground. I have vivid memories of this school and its teachers. Apart from one female teacher in the first class all the staff were men who, I believe, had been there for most of their teaching careers. The style of instruction was formalised in the extreme with everyone sitting in rows facing the teacher and the blackboard and with a heavy bias to the three Rs. The chanting of multiplication tables has stood me in good stead to this day. We were taught some history and geography and occasionally we were allowed to indulge in some craft work. One facet of the curriculum that seems to have gone the way of the Dodo was class-singing and music instruction in tonic sol-fa notation. The master used the prescribed hand signals and we all followed his instructions chanting Doh, re, me, etc.

Most adults in the town referred to Pentrepoeth school as 'The Lancy' since it was established originally in 1813 as a Lancasterian school, named after the Victorian education pioneer Joseph Lancaster. The solid red brick school, built in 1896, that I attended in the 1930s had long abandoned Lancaster's monitorial system of instruction (whereby the older children taught the younger ones), but there was still a vestige with older boys, called monitors, performing classroom duties, such as filling up inkwells in the two-seater desks. The school building incorporated a small room known to us all by the mysterious name of 'The Board Room'. My chief recollection of this place was that it was where we were given magic lantern slide shows in the week preceding Christmas. Crammed in to this small room, which was never opened up to us on any other occasion, we were treated to hand-drawn and coloured slides of *Peter Pan* or *A Christmas Carol* projected from a large mahogany projector with a running commentary from one of the masters.

A memory of that era was the appearance in school of the attendance officer, or 'whipper-in', a Mr Cairns (pronounced in our household as Curns). He invariably sported bicycle clips on his trousers as the bicycle was his usual method of touring the town looking for truants, but I was told that he also had a motor-cycle and side-car which was often used to transport miscreants back to the school premises. To be threatened with Mr Cairns was a very effective way of getting me out of bed on the rare occasions when I fancied a day off school.

Most of the schoolyard games that we played as children during break-times and dinner times now seem lost to present generations. They varied with the seasons: conkers was obviously played in the autumn and marbles were a summer time activity. The bowling of hoops, both wooden and iron, was popular, the iron ones making a very satisfactory clatter on the tarmac, and the whipping of tops seemed to come round regularly in the winter-time. I'm sure that the tops were highly dangerous as they flew around like bullets, often breaking windows.

One aspect of the life of the town that erupted every week with regularity was the driving of herds of cattle from the town mart to the sidings of the railway station below Parade Road where cattle wagons awaited them. Motor transport of livestock was in its infancy and the railways reigned supreme. Pentrepoeth school was on the route taken by these cattle and their bellowing, coupled with the shouting of the drovers, has remained a vivid memory. This disruption to the school and town, as well as the mess that was left on the streets, only ceased with the closure of the railway sidings in the 1960s.

The outbreak of the war in 1939 is quite clear in my mind. Although we were then living in King Street, we often had Sunday dinner with my grand parents in their Quay Street house. I distinctly remember the solemn mood that prevailed following the 11a.m. broadcast on the radio by Neville Chamberlain and the subdued dinner that followed. In school precautions against air raids were immediately taken: one of the first exercises was to determine who would be allowed to go home if an alert was sounded. Those who lived very near to school, including myself, after taking a timed run home and back, were judged to be close enough to be able make a dash for home. Fortunately, I don't think we ever had to make the run. Another evacuation exercise had the whole school sitting, three or four to a step, on the massive stone stairs leading to the upper storeys – the reasoning being, I suppose, that this was the safest place in the building!

Everyone was obliged to carry a gas mask wherever they went, for masks had been distributed to the general population several months previously. To assist in their distribution, members of the ARP (Air Raid Precautions) spent a long time assembling them from the component parts and putting them in their boxes. I went with my father, a member of the ARP, on numerous occasions to a large room above Montague Burton's shop on the corner of King Street and Queen

Pentrepoeth school.

Street, where all this activity was going on. I still have my gas mask in its cardboard box covered with an oil cloth cover that my mother thoughtfully made for it so that it shouldn't get wet in the rain. The ARP wardens were installed in posts scattered around the town and post No. 8 was constructed in a basement room of our house in King Street. It was equipped with two bunks, an oil heater and an antiquated candlestick telephone. For several years this post was occupied every night by two wardens, who were to patrol the town every time the air-raid siren on top of St Peter's church tower was sounded. My mother as part of her war effort joined the ARP as a warden along with many others.

Over the course of the next four years the town changed in a way that, with hindsight, now seems a tremendous upheaval. The blackout of all street lights and all shop-window displays was immediate, and houses and public buildings had to provide thick curtains or shutters so that no chink of light could be seen. The shops also went to elaborate lengths to cover their doors with draped curtains or double doors that you had to fight your way through to gain entry. The few cars that were allowed to run had miniscule headlights, which slowed them to a crawl on dark nights. My mother often related the tale of going 200 yards from our door to the GPO in King Street to post a letter one moonless night and getting so hopelessly lost on the return that she had to be rescued by a passer-by who happened to have a torch.

Everyone was enjoined to paste strips of paper over their windows to prevent flying glass from bomb blast, and public buildings gradually built up massive sandbag walls to give them some protection. A further addition to the street scene was the creation of several large emergency water supply tanks on open spaces for the use of the newly formed Auxiliary Fire Service in case the water mains were broken by bombs. I remember a particularly large example opposite Elliston Terrace with the large letters EWS on each side!

The amiable inactivity that had constituted the life of the town in pre-war days came to an abrupt end with the arrival of the first of many contingents of troops that were billeted here for various periods. The barracks on Picton Terrace were immediately occupied as were several sheds and garages – in fact any building that could accommodate hastily cobbled together bunks and rudimentary cook houses. There was one of these establishments in Woods Row near our house and the days were alive with squads of soldiers marching to and from meals, the intervals being filled with much peeling of potatoes. To give a little relief to the populace and to provide an alternative to the pubs, the YMCA (Young Men's Christian Association) and the NAAFI (Navy, Army and Air Force Institute) opened clubs in the main streets with cafés and rough-and-ready sleeping quarters. Both these establishments were to remain going full blast until the end of the war. The small Borough Police Force (twelve in number) was naturally overwhelmed by this influx, and a shop in King Street was occupied by a Military Police detachment to assist in keeping order. They occupied themselves during the day with a billiard table (the click of the balls was a good give-away), only sallying forth in the evening and at weekends when any inebriated soldiers had to be rounded up.

Following Dunkirk in 1940 many foreign troops arrived in the town. The first were the Belgians, who were quartered in the Barracks (not the present building but the older Victorian structure that stood on the same spot). To accommodate local sensitivities all the public toilets were at once labelled *Dames* and *Messieurs*. Several of these Belgian soldiers married local girls and later brought up families in the town. Since the Belgians had Flemish names, I would surmise that the French toilet notices were slightly off key.

My mother, Edith Lodwick, in her ARP uniform in 1941.

The next contingent to arrive were Polish, and I should think that they were those who were allowed to come west by Stalin after Hitler's attack on Russia in 1941. Quite a number who could not return to their homeland after the war settled down as farmers in the Carmarthenshire countryside.

Late in 1943 American forces arrived in order to build a hospital on the site where the West Wales Hospital now stands. These men were mostly technical and medical personnel who made a much greater impact on the town than earlier arrivals. One reason was that they had a lot more money to spend, although there was not much on which to spend it. Many local girls became engaged to members of the US forces and some weddings did eventually ensue. The hospital was built to cater for the large number of casualties expected following the invasion of Europe; fortunately such casualties did not occur as foreseen and the camp at Glangwili was then surrounded with barbed wire and used to house German prisoners. Another camp was built on the Ystrad fields in Johnstown.

A development in 1943 was the armistice with Italy. This meant that all the Italian POWs, who had been mostly rounded up in Egypt, were kitted out with brown uniforms with a badge on the shoulder saying Italy, and set to work on the land. In Carmarthenshire this meant driving them around the countryside and dropping them off at any farms that needed workers. Some are there to this day – having declined a return home to sunnier climes!

A final chapter in this tale of war-time Carmarthen follows the ending of the war when, after a decent interval, the POW camps were opened up and German officers (but only officers) were allowed to perambulate the town. As I remember it, they were all polite and well-kitted out in their uniforms and on entering my parents' shop there was a lot of heel clicking; but unlike the Americans who had a lot of money, the Germans had none. I must not forget that there were also thousands of British troops who were in transit or billeted in the town – and you do not have to look very far to recognise the Scottish and Irish names that exist in Carmarthen today, following wartime marriages.

Our home life during wartime does not have sad or difficult memories for me for, unlike my parents, I was insulated from most of the horrors. I certainly remember the red glow in the sky from the burning of Swansea town centre following a heavy air raid, and reports of the bombing of Pembroke Dock soon filtered back – the wireless news reports, like the newspapers, were vague or positively misleading in certain respects. Likewise, the odd traveller from London would give us graphic accounts of the Blitz, and a Jewish Austrian refugee woman, who was billeted with us for some months, related stories of concentration camps which I'm sure my parents did not, at that time, take seriously. She had been in Vienna and seen Hitler himself when he made his triumphant entry into that city. I well remember her finding a German station on the wireless broadcasting a speech by Hitler, which she was able to translate for us verbatim.

Early in the war my parents had been asked by an aunt in Toronto if they wanted to send me to Canada for the 'duration'. The offer was declined, which was just as well as the ship on which I would have sailed (the *Benares Star*) was sunk by a U-boat with much loss of life. This same relation sent us food parcels during the war, and the excitement in opening them was only exceeded by the delight in consuming the contents which always included chocolates (that had completely disappeared from shops in town). Tropical fruits, such as bananas and oranges, were also completely missing for the whole of the war and many people grumbled that the cigarettes, which did not contain any Virginia tobacco, were not worth smoking! The miniscule rations of essential foods was always a problem, but I now believe we were all a lot healthier for having a diet that was practically devoid of fats and sugar. The coming of peace did not change the situation appreciably for some time, since these luxuries only returned to the shops very slowly.

Looking back, my life was very simple when compared with that of today's youngsters. However, the enjoyable times, which I certainly experienced, were then all the more keenly appreciated.

Victor G. Lodwickz

School days

Since moving back to live in Llansteffan I have come to realize that some of the newer villagers and indeed some who have resided here for a long while have assumed that the old school closed as the new one opened. This was not the situation; the old school fell into disrepair before the new one was built.

During the in-between years, the infants and the next class up were housed in the Memorial Hall. Screens were used to separate the two classes. The two classes were in the care of two female teachers. The eleven-plus class and the one below were accommodated in Moriah chapel vestry. These classes were in the charge of the headmaster, Mr C.D. Evans, and Mr Jeremy, who was succeeded by Mr Neil Davies. We spent happy days in the vestry and the examination results were excellent.

Early in the morning, if the weather was dry, some of us would wait on the bridge to welcome Mr Davies off the bus. We would then proceed up to the vestry. If it rained, we waited in the old school. The top classroom of the old school was used as the school kitchen and the bottom classroom was where we ate our dinner. The large room was out of bounds, as rain came through the roof and the floorboards were rotten. Mrs Davies was the cook and an elderly man called Joe did the odd jobs. In the morning, before school, Mrs Davies would prepare a tray of plastic beakers and a jug of milk. The milk had been delivered by Mr Harry Jones, the stores. Two of the older girls would carry the tray and jug up to the vestry for our consumption mid-morning. One morning we dropped the tray and the beakers rolled all over the road. We quickly gathered them up. Of course we did not know that several had cracked. This became apparent later when Mr Evans poured out the milk. It leaked down onto the floor and we were crestfallen. Needless to say, the headmaster was not amused.

The little room in the old school where we ate dinner was heated by a good coal fire, which was protected by a sturdy fireguard. Both teachers sat at a small table and the boys at one trestle and the girls at another. When we asked Mrs Davies what would be for dinner, she always replied, 'Bees' knees and elephants' toenails.' On one occasion she flavoured the cawl with sage. Several of us were not happy and left most of it. On the way out she asked why we had only eaten a little. When we said that we did not like the sage she said, 'Right, never again, and what do you want for pudding tomorrow?'

On winter mornings when we waited in the old school for Mr Evans to unlock the Vestry, we sat around the fireguard enjoying the heat from the fire. One morning a boy decided to sweep inside the fireguard. The broom caught fire, he quickly ran with it to the lobby. The brush-head was burnt out. We dreaded Mr Evans finding out. The day was saved by Mrs Davies, who came rushing to us on hearing our shouts. She took it from us and told us never to play with fire again.

When the school doctor visited, we were examined in the little room. It was warm and cosy in front of the fire. While the girls were being attended to, the boys played in the yard.

From time to time there would be shrieks of alarm from the girls because the boys would be jumping up to try looking through the window. There was an old school bell outside and a piece of wire was attached to it to pull it backwards and forwards. While jumping up to the window, the boys would tug on the wire and the bell would ring. These interruptions into the girls' medicals would bring Mr Evans outside the school to deal with the boys.

Of course the headmaster spent time down in the Memorial Hall with the younger children. Their dinner was brought down from the kitchen in the old school by Mr Harry Jones. He packed the metal containers into his little three-wheeled cart.

On some occasions Miss Betty Wyatt would sent the eldest boy up to the Vestry to get Mr Evans as his presence was required to deal with the misdemeanours of some of the boys. I remember watching Mr Evans on these occasions donning his coat and hat and finally picking up his cane and slipping it up his sleeve. He would say, 'The magic wand, the sight of it works wonders.'

On Friday afternoons the girls walked down to the Hall for sewing lessons with Miss Wyatt. The boys remained for art. In the summer term we went to the Green. The girls played rounders, and the boys football. Sometimes the boys went out cockling and digging bait with Mr Evans, while the girls lazed in the rock pools.

At the end of the summer term the local policeman would visit school and give us a safety talk to enable us to remain safe while playing around the village in the holidays. He came again before Christmas. This talk would include the danger to the elderly in particular when we made the pavements dangerous by repeatedly sliding along in icy conditions.

On one occasion while we were at our lessons, the Vestry door flew open and Mr Jack Williams, Plasgwyn, appeared in the doorway. He was looking for the policeman. A plane on a training flight had burst into flames and crashed onto one of the fields of Down Farm. Later that day we children accompanied by some adults made our way to the field. The pieces of metal were strewn about. By then the RAF officials were present. Some of the boys took small pieces of metal home, much to the discomfort of their mothers. We were all sad to hear that the pilot had been killed. I believe he was Pilot Officer Brown. Fortunately for us he brought the plane down into a field and away from Llansteffan and Llanybri. This was a day when a shadow passed over our happy, sunny schooldays.

Heather Chamber.

Atgofion crwtyn ysgol o dref Caerfyrddin cyn ac yn ystod yr Ail Ryfel Byd

Yn Ysgol Plant Bach Pentrepoeth y dechreuodd fy nyddiau ysgol i, ac er imi wybod bron yn sicr mai oedolyn wnaeth fy nhywys i'r adeilad ym 1935, bellach does gennyf ddim atgof o'r daith fer honno o'm cartref yn Heol y Cei. Yn y dyddiau hynny yr oedd trefn a rheolaeth bendant ar wersi hyd yn oed yn nosbarth y babanod, gyda llawer o ganu a llafarganu, a phob un yn eistedd mewn rhesi taclus gan wynebu'r athro. Gydol misoedd yr haf, cofiaf yn glir yr adlen gynfas a fyddai'n cael ei chodi ar ran o'r iard chwarae fel modd o gynnal gwersi yn yr awyr agored - hyn mae'n debyg i gyd-fynd â'r theori ar y pryd bod digonedd o awyr iach yn rhwystro amryw glefydau megis y ddarfodedigaeth. Doedd dim dwywaith amdani bod cartrefi rhai o'r plant mewn cyflwr aflan, fel y gwelwyd bob dydd o gwmpas yr ardal.

Pan oeddwn yn saith, symudwyd fy nosbarth i'r ysgol Plant Iau drws nesa' ble cawsom ni ein gwahanu: y bechgyn i fyny'r grisiau gyda iard chwarae'n wynebu Heol y Berllan, a'r merched lawr llawr yn cael defnydd o iard chwarae Heol Dwr Fach. Mae gennyf atgofion byw o'r ysgol hon a'i hathrawon. Heblaw un athrawes fenywaidd yn y dosbarth cyntaf, dynion oedd y gweddill a oedd wedi treulio'r rhan fwyaf o'u gyrfa dysgu yno, am wn i. Roedd natur yr hyfforddi yn llym iawn, gyda phawb yn eistedd mewn rhesi'n wynebu'r athro a'r bwrdd du, gyda phwyslais mawr at y tair R. Gwir yw dweud bod llafarganu'r tablau lluosi wedi bod yn help mawr imi hyd heddiw. Cawsom ambell wers Hanes a Daearyddiaeth, ac o bryd i'w gilydd byddem yn cael mwynhau ychydig o gelf a chrefft. Un ffased o'r cwricwlwm, sydd wedi hen farw bellach, oedd canu yn y dosbarth a chael gwersi cerddoriaeth gan ddefnyddio nodiant y tonic sol-ffa. Byddai'r meistr yn defnyddio'r arwyddion llaw penodedig, a ninnau'n dilyn ei gyfarwyddiadau wrth ganu do, re, mi, etc.

I'r rhan fwyaf o oedolion y dref, *Y Lancy* oedd yr enw ar ysgol Pentrepoeth am iddi gael ei sefydlu'n wreiddiol ym 1813 fel ysgol Lancastraidd, wedi ei henwi ar ôl yr arloeswr addysg Fictorianaidd, Joseph Lancaster. Yr oedd yr ysgol o friciau coch, ac fe'i hadeiladwyd ym 1813. Roedd yr ysgol honno a roddodd fy addysg gynradd i mi yn yr 1930au wedi hen ymadael â system fonitoraidd Lancaster o addysgu (ble gwelwyd y plant hyn yn dysgu'r rhai iau) ond yr oedd olion ohono'n dal i'w gweld gyda'r bechgyn hyn, y *monitors*, wrth iddynt gael swyddi o fewn y dosbarth, megis llenwi'r potiau inc yn y desgiau i ddau. Wedi ei hymgorffori yn adeilad yr ysgol oedd ystafell fechan a elwid am ryw reswm dirgel i bawb, *The Board Room*. Fy atgof pennaf o'r ystafell hon yw'r wythnos cyn y Nadolig ble byddem ni wedi ein gwasgu i mewn, bob un, i weld y sioeau sleid hudlusern. Fyddai'r ystafell byth yn cael ei hagor ar achlysur arall, ond dyna'r lle'r oeddem ni bob Nadolig, yn gwylio gwledd o luniau lliwgar *Peter Pan* a *A Christmas Carol*, oll wedi eu peintio gyda llaw ar y gwahanol sleidiau, ac yn swn yr athro'n adrodd y stori, byddai'r taflunydd mahogani'n arddangos y lluniau hardd ar y wal o'n blaen.

Atgof arall o'r cyfnod hwnnw oedd golwg Mr Cairns (neu Curns fel byddai'n teulu ni yn ei alw), swyddog presenoldeb yr ysgol, neu'r '*whipper-in*'. Yn ddieithriad byddai'n dod i'r gwaith yn gwisgo clipiau beic am ei drowsus, am mai ar ei feic y byddai fel arfer yn crwydro'r dref yn chwilio am blant ar grwydr, er imi glywed unwaith fod ganddo feic-modur yn ogystal â seidcar ynghlwm wrth hwnnw i gludo'r dihirod yn ôl i gyffiniau'r ysgol. Roedd y bygythiad hwn gan Mr Cairns yn ffordd effeithiol iawn o sicrhau fy mod yn codi gyda'r bore, y troeon anghyffredin hynny pan fyddwn wedi hoffi cael diwrnod adre'.

Mae'r rhan fwyaf o'r gemau y byddem ni wedi eu chwarae allan ar yr iard wedi hen farw erbyn hyn. Byddent yn amrywio fesul tymor: roedd concyrs yn cael ei chwarae'n amlwg yn yr Hydref, a gyda'r haf byddai marblys yn hen ffefryn. Roedd chwarae gyda chylch a bachyn, rhai pren a rhai haearn yn boblogaidd, yn enwedig wrth i'r rhai haearn wneud twrw buddugoliaethus ar y llawr tarmac, heb anghofio troi topiau a fu'n ffefryn gyda'r gaeaf. Prin ei bod hi'n anodd dadlau fod y topiau'n beryg wrth iddynt hedfan o gwmpas y lle fel tân gwyllt, gan dorri sawl ffenestr yn y broses.

Agwedd o Gaerfyrddin a ychwanegodd at fwrlwm prysur y dref yn wythnosol oedd y dasg o yrru haid o wartheg i lawr o'r farchnad hyd at gilffyrdd yr orsaf drenau o dan Heol y Rhodfa ble byddai'r wagenni gwartheg yn aros amdanynt. Roedd y dull o gludo gwartheg gan ddefnyddio cerbydau modur yn weddol newydd yn y dref, gyda'r rheilffyrdd yn arglwyddiaethu bob tro. Mae sn aflafar brefu'r gwartheg a gweiddi'r porthmyn yn fyw yn fy nghof hyd heddiw, wrth gofio eu gweld yn mynd heibio i'r ysgol ar eu taith wythnosol o'r farchnad. Er i'r ddefod hon dorri ar draws llonyddwch y dref a thynnu sylw sawl plentyn ysgol, ni ddaeth diwedd arni nes i gilffyrdd yr orsaf drenau gau yn yr 1960au.

Erys dechrau Rhyfel 1939 yn glir yn fy nghof. Er i'n cartref fod yn Stryd y Brenin ar y pryd, byddem yn aml yn treulio dydd Sul yn nh fy mam-gu a ´nhad-cu yn Stryd y Cei i gael cinio. Cofiaf un tro'n enwedig, wedi i Neville Chamberlain ddatgan Rhyfel am 11yb, a'r cinio distaw a ddilynodd. Cymerwyd rhagofalon yn erbyn ymosodiadau o'r awyr yn syth yn yr ysgol. Un o'r profion cyntaf a wnaethpwyd oedd gweld pwy fyddai'n cael mynd adref pe bai rhybudd yn cael ei seinio. Bu'n rhaid i minnau a'r plant hynny a oedd yn byw yn agos i gyffiniau'r ysgol redeg o'r ysgol i'n cartrefi ac yn ôl, gan weld a oeddem yn gallu gwneud hynny mewn digon o amser. Yn ffodus, ni fu'n rhaid inni fyth wneud y daith honno. Mewn ymarfer gwacàu arall, gwelwyd yr ysgol i gyd yn eistedd, yn dri neu'n bedwar i bob gris, ar y grisiau carreg enfawr a arweiniai at loriau uchaf yr ysgol - y rheswm am hyn, mae'n sir, oedd mai dyma'r llecyn mwyaf diogel yn yr adeilad!

Yr oedd hi'n orfodol i bawb gario mwgwd nwy ble bynnag yr âi, ar ôl i'r mygydau gael eu dosbarthu i'r boblogaeth gyffredinol fisoedd ynghynt. I helpu gyda'r dosraniad yma, treuliodd aelodau o'r ARP (Rhagofalon Cyrch Awyr) dipyn o amser yn cydosod y darnau cydrannol a'u rhoi yn eu blychau. Euthum sawl gwaith gyda 'nhad, a oedd yn aelod o'r ARP, i ystafell fawr uwchben siop *Montague Burton* ar gornel Stryd y Brenin a Stryd y Frenhines, ble byddai hyn oll yn digwydd. Mae'r masg nwy dal gyda mi hyd heddiw, yn daclus yn ei flwch wedi ei orchuddio â'r clwtyn olew a roddodd fy mam drosto rhag iddo wlychu yn y glaw. Cafodd y wardeiniau ARP eu sefydlu mewn gwahanol safleoedd o gwmpas y dref, a safle rhif 8 wedi'i lleoli yn seler ein ty yn Stryd y Brenin. Yn yr ystafell hon yr oedd dau wely bync, gwresogydd olew, a theleffon hynafol canhwyllbrenaidd. Llenwyd y swydd liw nos am flynyddoedd gan ddau warden a gerddai'r strydoedd bob tro y byddai seiren cyrch awyr yn cael ei seinio o dop twr Eglwys San Pedr.Ymunodd fy mam, fel rhan o'i hymroddiad i'r rhyfel, gyda'r ARP fel warden ynghyd â sawl un arall.

O edrych yn ôl dros y pedair blynedd a ddilynai, gwelwyd y dref yn newid mewn modd dramatig tu hwnt. Diffoddwyd goleuadau'r strydoedd yn syth, ynghyd â chael gwared ar yr arddangosfeydd yn ffenestri'r siopau, a bu'n rhaid i dai ac adeiladau cyhoeddus osod llenni trwchus neu gaeadau dros eu ffenestri fel na fyddai'r mymryn lleiaf o olau'n gallu cael ei weld. Cymerodd y siopau fesurau llym gan orchuddio'u drysau â llenni neu trwy gael drysau dwbl a fyddai'n gadael i ddyn ymladd ei ffordd i mewn i'r siop. Byddai goleuadau-blaen bychain ar yr ychydig geir a fyddai'n cael eu caniatáu i yrru ar hyd y strydoedd ond yn peri i'r ceir orfod cropian yn araf ar noson dywyll. Byddai fy mam yn aml yn cofio'r tro pan gerddodd 200 llath un noson dywyll o ddrws y ty i'r Swyddfa Bost yn Stryd y Brenin i bostio llythyr, ac yn gorfod cael ei hachub ar y ffordd adre gan rywun oedd yn cario fflachlamp am iddi golli ei ffordd yn llwyr yn y gwyll.

Gorchmynnwyd i bawb bastio stribedi o bapur dros eu ffenestri i atal gwydr rhag tasgu pe bai bom yn ffrwydro, ac yn raddol cododd adeiladau cyhoeddus wal o fagiau tywod o'u blaenau i'w diogelu. Rhywbeth arall a wnaethpwyd ar y strydoedd oedd creu tanciau cyflenwad dwr mewn argyfwng ar lecynnau agored, at ddefnydd y Gwasanaeth Tân Cynorthwyol a oedd newydd ei sefydlu, pe bai cyflenwad dwr yn cael ei dorri gan ffrwydriadau. Cofiaf un enghraifft go fawr yn benodol gyferbyn â Theras Elliston gyda'r llythrennau EWS ar bob ochr!

Torrwyd ar lonyddwch hamddenol y dyddiau cyn y rhyfel yn sydyn gyda dyfodiad y cyntaf o sawl mintai o filwyr a gafodd eu biledu ar amryw o gyfnodau. Cafodd y barics yn Heol Picton eu meddiannu'n syth ynghyd â sawl garej a sied - a dweud y gwir, unrhyw adeilad a fedrai gymhwyso gwelyau bync wedi eu rhoi at ei gilydd ar frys a thai coginio elfennol. Bu un o'r sefydliadau hyn yn Rhes Wood ar bwys ein ty ni, a dyddiau prysur oedd y rheiny gyda sgwadiau o filwyr ar gyrch yn ôl ac ymlaen o ginio, a'r cyfnodau rhwng y bwyta'n cael eu llenwi â chrafu tatws. I gynnig ychydig o ryddhad i'r werin yn ogystal â bod yn ddewis gwahanol i'r tafarnau, agorodd yr YMCA (Cymdeithas Gristnogol Dynion Ifanc) a'r NAAFI (Sefydliad y Llynges, Byddin, a'r Llu Awyr) glybiau ym mhrif strydoedd y dref, a fyddai'n cynnwys caffis ac aneddau blith draphlith. Yr oedd y ddau sefydliad yma i barhau yn gryf tan ddiwedd y rhyfel. Yn naturiol, gorlethwyd yr Heddlu Plwyfol (12 mewn nifer) gyda'r dylifiad yma, a meddiannwyd siop yn Stryd y Brenin gan garfan o'r Heddlu Milwrol, i helpu cadw trefn. Gan dreulio oriau'r dydd o gwmpas bwrdd biliards (yn sn clicio'r peli) byddent yn cyrchu oddi yno ond ar benwythnosau neu nosweithiau pan fyddai angen casglu milwyr meddw ynghyd.

Yn dilyn Dunkirk ym 1940 cyrhaeddodd minteioedd tramor i'r dref. Y Belgiaid oedd y cyntaf i gyrraedd ac ymgartrefu yn y Barics (nid yn yr adeilad presennol ond yr un Fictorianaidd hyn a saif ar yr un safle). Labelwyd y toiledau ar unwaith gyda *Dames* a *Messieurs* mewn ymgais i addasu'r dref yn unol â theimladau lleol. Priododd llawer o'r milwyr Belgaidd â merched lleol gan fagu teuluoedd yn y dref yn hwyrach. Ac am mai enwau Fflemeg oedd gan y Belgiaid, nid oedd y labeli Ffrengig yma'n taro deuddeg.

Y dyrfa nesaf o filwyr a gyrhaeddodd oedd y Pwyliaid, a thybiaf mai'r rhai hynny wnaeth Stalin adael iddynt ddod tua'r gorllewin oeddynt, wedi ymosodiad Hitler ar Rwsia ym 1941. Ymgartrefodd sawl un na allai ddychwelyd adref ar ôl i'r rhyfel ostegu, fel ffermwyr yn ardaloedd gwledig y Sir.

Yn ddiweddar ym 1943 gwelwyd lluoedd o'r Unol Daleithiau yn cyrraedd y dref i adeiladu ysbyty ar union safle Ysbyty Gorllewin Cymru heddiw. Personél Technegol a Meddygol oedd y rhan fwyaf o'r dynion hyn, ac effeithiwyd gryn dipyn ar y dref wedi eu dyfodiad. Un rheswm am hyn oedd bod mwy o arian ganddynt i wario, er nad oedd llawer y gellid ei brynu, chwaith. Gwelwyd sawl merch leol ac aelodau o luoedd UDA yn dyweddïo, gyda sawl un yn llwyddo i briodi. Adeiladwyd yr ysbyty er mwyn y nifer helaeth o gleifion disgwyliedig yn dilyn ymosodiad Ewrop; yn ffodus ni bu'r angen am gymorth o'r fath, ac yn hytrach amgylchynwyd y gwersyll yng Nglangwili gyda weiren adfach a bu'r adeilad yn gartref i garcharorion Almaenaidd. Adeiladwyd gwersyll arall ar gaeau'r Ystrad yn Nhre Ioan.

Y datblygiad nesaf oedd y cadoediad gyda'r Eidal ym 1943. Golygai hyn y byddai'r Carcharorion Rhyfel o'r Eidal, a oedd wedi eu casglu ynghyd yn yr Aifft, yn cael gwisgoedd brown â bathodyn ar yr ysgwydd yn dweud 'Yr Eidal', a gwnaethpwyd iddynt weithio ar y tir. Yng nghyd-destun Sir Gaerfyrddin, yr oedd hyn yn golygu gyrru'r milwyr o gwmpas y wlad ac yna eu gadael ar bob fferm a fyddai'n ddiolchgar o gael cymorth. Mae rhai ohonynt yno hyd heddiw – wedi gwrthod cynnig i ddychwelyd adref at dywydd gwell!

Mae pennod olaf yr hanes hwn am Gaerfyrddin gydol y rhyfel yn dilyn terfyn yr ymladd pan agorwyd wersylloedd y carcharorion, wedi hir oedi, a bodlonwyd i'r swyddogion Almaenig (a'r rheiny yn unig) gerdded o gwmpas y dref. Hyd eithaf fy ngof, yr oeddynt yn ddigon serchog yn edrych yn drwsiadus yn eu gwisgoedd brown gyda'u sodlau'n clicio wrth ddod i mewn i siop fy rhieni; ond prin oedd arian yr Almaenwyr yn wahanol i'r Americanwyr cefnog. Heb anghofio wrth gwrs am y miloedd o filwyr Prydeinig oedd ar daith neu wedi eu biledu yn y dref - a prin nad oes angen chwilio ymhell cyn dod ar draws yr enwau Albanaidd a Gwyddelig sy'n bodoli yng Nghaerfyrddin heddiw, yn dilyn priodasau adeg y rhyfel.

Cadwyd fi rhag y rhan fwyaf o'r erchyllderau gydol y rhyfel ac nid nid cyfnod anodd ydoedd i mi felly, yn wahanol i'r hyn y bu'n rhaid i fy rhieni ymdopi ag ef wrth gwrs. Mae'r atgof o weld yr awyr tanbaid yn glir yn fy nghof, ble'r oedd canol tref Abertawe'n fflam wedi cyrch awyr enfawr, a chofio clywed sôn am y bomio yn Noc Penfro - yr adroddiadau Newyddion, fel y papurau newydd, yn amwys neu'n gamarweiniol iawn mewn sawl agwedd. Yn yr un modd, byddai ambell i deithiwr o Lundain yn rhoi adroddiadau byw o'r bomio ac adroddodd ffoadures Iddewig o Awstria, a oedd wedi ei biledu atom ni am dri mis, hanes y gwersylloedd crynhoi inni, er i mi fod yn sicr nad oedd fy rhieni wedi cymryd fawr o sylw o'r straeon hynny ar y pryd. Bu hithau yn Vienna a gwelodd Hitler ei hun pan aeth i mewn i'r ddinas honno'n fuddigoliaethus. Rwy'n cofio'n glir iddi ddarganfod gorsaf Almaeneg ar y radio yn darlledu un o areithiau Hitler, gan ei chyfieithu inni air am air.

Yn nyddiau cynnar y rhyfel cynigiodd fy modryb yn Toronto i'm rhieni f'anfon i Ganada am weddill y cyfnod hwnnw. Gwrthodwyd y cynnig, a gorau oll am hynny, pan glywais am suddo'r cwch y byddem wedi hwylio arni (y *Benares Star*)

The Wings for Victory Parade in Guildhall Square. 1943.

gan long danfor gyda sawl un yn marw. Byddai'r berthynas hon hefyd yn danfon parseli o fwyd atom gydol y rhyfel, a ninnau'n eu hagor yn llawn cynnwrf yn awchu am y siocledi (a oedd erbyn hyn wedi llwyr ddiflannu o siopau'r dref). Doedd dim sôn chwaith am ffrwythau trofannol yn y dre, megis bananas ac orennau, a bu sawl cwyn nad oedd y sigarennau'n werth eu hysmygu, am nad oeddynt yn cynnwys baco *Virginia*. Roedd y dognau pitw o'r bwydydd hanfodol yn broblem, ond erbyn hyn rwy'n credu i ni fod yn llawer iachach bryd hynny, a ninnau'n byw ar ddeiet heb fawr ddim braster na siwgr. Nid effeithiodd yr heddwch a ddaeth wedi'r rhyfel lawer ar ein deiet am gyfnod digon hir, gyda'r moethau'n dychwelyd i'r siopau yn ara' deg.

Wrth edrych nôl, bywyd digon cyffredin oedd fy mhlentyndod i o'i gymharu â bywydau pobl ifanc heddiw. Wedi dweud hynny, bu'r cyfnodau hapus y bûm i'n ddigon ffodus i'w cael, yn atgofion melys i'w trysori.

Victor G. Lodwick.

5 Health Care

Medical care in Carmarthen before the NHS

In 1948 the National Health Service started. Doctors did not welcome its coming. They felt they were managing very well without Government interference. Even during the war with all its difficulties, when they were very shorthanded – all young doctors were being called up to the Forces - they had worked hard and kept things going.

I came to Carmarthen in 1946 after serving as a Medical Officer in the Royal Air Force. My wife Nest had served in the Royal Army Medical Corps, but she was now working in Furnace House Surgery, assisting Dr Arwyn Davies and Dr Harold Lloyd. I did a six month refresher course in Morriston hospital and then I joined Furnace House. Harold Lloyd worked in the surgery for a further short time, and then he left to become a full time surgeon in the hospital. My wife left to become a clinic doctor, and Dr John Davies - Arwyn's son came out of the Royal Air Force and he, Arwyn and I became partners.

There were four other GPs in Carmarthen and they all had appointments at the hospital. The hospital had a Secretary Administrator with one assistant, and a junior doctor was in charge of the wards. A matron, Miss Hartland, was in charge of the nursing staff. Most of the surgery was done by Dr Harold Lloyd who was an experienced surgeon, and the midwifery by Dr J.R.E. James who had recently been a GP in Furnace House, but was a trained gynaecologist. A surgeon from Swansea, Mr Gabe, came once a week and performed a list of operations. A dermatologist from Swansea came to do a clinic. A lot of the hospital work was done by the GPs.

Dr Roland Webb was a capable surgeon and obstetrician, and looked after his own patients. Dr Parry ran the X-ray room. Dr Adam Lewis gave anesthetics, and Dr Lewis Davies of Morfa Lane looked after the staff, and also the long-stay patients in Penlan, which used to be the old workhouse.

The hospital was maintained by voluntary contributions, and patients had to pay for treatment, except some who contributed to a Medical Aid Fund. If patients couldn't afford to pay, then there were arrangements to accommodate them.

Outside the hospital, GPs had a list of panel patients, those who paid national health contributions at their work place, and who are covered for medical treatment. Their families were not covered and had to pay for private treatment provided they could afford it. In miming areas miners paid a contribution to their wages, which covered their families treatment. It might have been a good idea if this method of insurance payments had been adopted in the NHS, which would have given the service a better financial base.

In our surgery we had one receptionist, Miss Bessie Evans who ran the surgery. She took the telephone calls and did the dispensing from the stock bottles. She recorded the work and sent out the bills. She knew whether the patient could afford to pay the bill or not.

Dr John Davies and I worked amicably, and

we shared the work of the practice. We were on call the whole time apart from one half-day a week, and an occasional weekend with the family. Home visiting was the expected thing - we visited old patients regularly, even if they were not ill. I visited one old lady once a month for years to give her injection for her pernicious anaemia. Night calls were common - sometimes out in the wilds of the country.

I remember visiting a Polish lady with asthma on a farm I hadn't visited before. It was a terrible night, very dark, with wind and rain - water cascading down the country road, and the husband standing with a lantern at the turning to his farm I only just managed to see him. Home deliveries of babies was the thing - only first babies had prompt admission to the hospital. If forceps delivery was needed, it was done at home by the doctor with his partner giving the anaesthetic. Sometimes the nurse assisted.

GPs had to carry more responsibility than at present, as there was not the same consultant support, but there was a firm bond between doctor and patient. I look back with affection at those days, before 1948 before the NHS.

Dr John Crane.

Mushrooms, aspirin and Mata Hari

'You know where you are?' she asked.

I looked down the long, many-windowed room. Opposite me was a row of empty beds, neatly made, on my side there was one occupied bed with screens around it. I glanced behind me at the windows through which the July sun shone brightly. They were barred with black iron. 'Yes,' I said 'I know where I am.'

The day passed quietly, once a white-coated woman came and questioned me.

'Did you have a vision? Did you see Christ on his cross?'

I looked at her in astonishment. Did she think I was mad? Why should I see Christ?

'No' I said with conviction. 'I did not see Christ on his cross.'

Night came and the ward filled up with middle-aged women. The lights were dimmed but the night nurse sitting at a table at the top of the ward stood out under stronger light. She had a kind face. I watched her as she wrote quietly. When she looked up I asked her abruptly:

'What's your name?'

'Mata Hari,' she replied kindly.

The name sounded familiar but out of place. I had heard it before. Where? I kept watching her. People were funny. I thought of dogs and how constant and reliable they were. They did not lie or say unexpected things.

'Are there any dogs in this place?' I asked her cautiously.

'No,' she replied in reassuring tones, 'there are no dogs here.'

She seemed to think I was frightened of dogs, whereas I would have liked to have a dog to talk to and stroke. I gave up and went to sleep.

Sometime in the next three days clothes appeared.

'Come along,' said a brisk nurse with an ordinary name, 'You are going to another ward. To the Admission Unit.'

There were many buildings scattered around the large one I had just left, but we walked past them till we came to a one-storied modern looking one. The nurse led me along a wide corridor with a parquet floor and delivered me to sister who took me to a large sitting room. Here the women were in ordinary street clothes. None wore aprons. Some were middle-aged, some were no more than teenagers. I sat in a comfortable armchair. The patients in the first ward had been talkative; here some were silent, others talked quietly together. Strangely I decided that I preferred the first ward. Here no one said more than a few words to me.

I closed my eyes to shut out this strange new world, but I had to open them when a doctor came on his rounds. He asked some conventional questions making no mention of visions and passed on to the next woman. When he had gone I got up and started inspecting the room. There was a poster on the wall and I read it with interest. It said that if anyone felt that they were unjustly detained they were at liberty to contact their MP. I thought of Roderick Bowen, the liberal member for Cardiganshire. I had attended his meetings a couple of times when I was a student but the poster somehow seemed irrelevant. Interesting all the same. The next day I was taken 'to have my brain waves measured.' The technician chatted to the nurse about the disestablishment of the Church in Wales. Perhaps it was supposed to stimulate my brainwaves. That night I woke up in fear, my heart beating furiously. I can't remember the nightmare that caused the alarm, but some patients complained at being disturbed.

Perhaps it was because of the disturbance or my chat with the doctor but I was moved again. As before it was to a modern building, so new that one ward was still empty.

'You will have treatment,' they said.

I did but at the end of six weeks I felt no different and that was that. I did, however, solve the mystery of Mata Hari. When I remarked that the kind faced nurse never came to the ward I was now on they said 'You must mean Mair Tahany.'

So many mysteries have simple explanations.

I fell into the routine. It was a well-run place. Mornings were treatment time for those who might respond to it, housework for others; afternoons were occupational therapy. The hours between tea and supper were unstructured. Most patients went to bed at eight, the privileged few were allowed to watch TV until nine. There was a system of privileges. Town parole and home weekends were the apogee. The hospital canteen was popular with those who had money. One could buy Kit-Kats, cigarettes, coffee, biros and various odds and ends. Saturday and Wednesday afternoons were slightly different because those were visiting days. There were weekly films. I remember *The Great Escape* and *The Bridge over the River Kwai.* Once we went to Swansea to see a pantomime. Very long stay patients had summer holidays somewhere by the sea. A male nurse came to run Housie-housie (a version of Bingo) in the day room once a week. There were dances but I couldn't dance and never went to one. Most patients were encouraged to the point of coercion to go to church but I was told I didn't have to go. I asked was it because I had religious mania I didn't have to attend, but Sister said no, I didn't have religious mania. I found it all puzzling but made the best of it.

Church going was interesting. The congregation was mixed and came from many wards. There were two chaplains. The vicar was an expert on bees. I had seen him in a bee-keeping exhibition with bees crawling all over his bare arms in a friendly fashion. Nothing seemed to ruffle him. His non-conformist colleague looked very serious. He was the librarian and I decided I didn't want any books. Once a man made strange noises during a sermon and had to be taken out. The sermons were nondescript and we always sang the same hymns. The favourite seemed to be 'Can a mother's tender care, cease towards the child she bare?' My friend urged me to take communion but I never did.

We learnt to knit, to tat, to crochet, to make rugs, to make quilted cushions. Sometimes a hairdresser came and we went to have our hair done. This was considered very modern. I regretted complaining of toothache. There was no talk of fillings, you had toothache and your tooth was removed and that was that. I still have an occasional twinge in the region from which that tooth was removed.

Curiosity is a quality that dies hard. I volunteered to go to a workroom for long term patients. It meant going to the main building and having pocket money. I felt a rich woman being able to buy odds and ends in the canteen. My friend and I carried clothes to the laundry and medical specimens to the laboratory. We were also given town parole but alarm bells rang when we innocently accepted a lift back from Trinity College students from across the way. Life was disciplined but had a childlike security. It was degrading to have one's baths supervised and to have no bolts on the toilet doors, but one got accustomed to everything.

Long-term patients didn't often see doctors apart from the annual medical examination. There was however a Sunday ward inspection by the chief doctor or deputy. There were often enquiries, – 'When am I going home?' – that received non-committal answers. Some went home for weekends seemingly 'On Approval', and came back with nothing changed. I never asked to go home. When I saw the iron bars I accepted that I was there for good. It was an escape from many problems to be here with a security of sorts. But the outside world had not finished with me. People who I had never expected to see again visited on various pretexts like: 'I am going abroad as a missionary and won't be in Wales again for years.'

One thing led to another and I found myself outside after nearly two years. A lot of things had changed during those years but one thing was unchanged. No one told the exact reason why I was admitted and I didn't feel much different. I had simply learnt to live with things I didn't understand.

Mushrooms and aspirins? On the night before I slid into a coma I had mushrooms for supper then swallowed too many aspirins and vomited them up. At some time I came to and saw a green vine tree climbing the walls of my room. It was a very calming and peaceful experience and it never occurred to me to mention that luxuriant vine tree in hospital. Had I accidentally eaten a magic mushroom? They never seemed to ask the right questions.

Nest Lloyd.

Ysbyty dewi sant (1956-1958)

Er chwilio yn y llwch
Yng nghoridorau hirion eu hymennydd
Ni fedrant afael yn y geiriau ddywedai
Pam na allant ganu'r gan yn gywir
Na dliyn patrwm dawns y cyfnod.

Yn y golchdy mae gwragedd tawel
a'u dwylo'n ddyddiol yn y golchion
ond ni all llif dyfroedd lawer
olchi bant y staen sy'n dwyno
patrymau cynhenid eu hymennydd.
Mae hen ofid yn mynnu crynhoi,
Hen archoll yn mynnau crawni.

Yn y gweithdy gludiwn ffigyrau papur
Ar galendrau i'n ffeiriau elusen,
Ond yma, a'r ystafell yn olau
a'r tan yn gynnes,
mae dyddiau a misoedd yn ddibwys.
Fel plant, rydym du allan I amser y byd..

Ffugiwn ddilyn defodau cymdeithas:
ffilmiau, bingo, dawnsiau wythnosol.
Yn syber, cerddwn I'r eglwys,
plygwn lin a chanu mawl i'r Ior,
ond does neb yn gofyn gair o'n profiad.
Ofnwn syrthio o ward i ward,
Disgyn grisiau hierarchaeth i'r gwaelod.
Fel plant safwn ar risiau troellog
yn sbecian lawr ar loriau is.
Yno ymrithia dawns cysgodion nwydwyllt.

Mae dychryn yn ein parlysu,
caewn ein cegau, plygwn ein pennau,
glanhawn, brodiwn, gwewn sgarffiau.

Myfyriaf ar nofelau am bobl drallodus
Yn gorwedd ar lythau'n ymateb
i gwestinynau cynnil holwr doeth.
Gollyngant eu beichiau yn yr ystafell dawel
wrth draed rhyw dad gyffeswr rhiniol,
yn rhydd cerddant allan I briffyrdd y byd.

Ond pe cawn chwilio'r coridorau I gyd
gwn na chawn yma ystafell tangnefedd.

Nest Lloyd.

6 Crime, Punishment and Beyond the Grave

Murder under Merlin's gaze

It's hard to imagine now these most tranquil byways, just one mile north of the little village of Whitemill in the Towy valley, were witness to an unfortunate murder. The story revealed itself to me slowly and in stages and began when my husband Roy told me our smallholding, which lies between Whitemill and Llanfihangel Uwch Gwili, had been a working corn grist mill until the 1940s. The very old Cornish and French millstones which now adorn my rockeries are, alas, mostly broken, but nevertheless are tangible evidence of the existence of the old mill. I became intrigued by the now vanished mill-race and mill building which are shown on our old deeds and was sad that the house name failed to reflect any reference to its former status as an important working mill. I subsequently discovered by trawling through the deeds that the mill was originally called Felin-Llainddu, which was known as Glanddu mill for a time and then reverted back to Llaniddu mill, a slightly anglicised version of its original title. Sometime after 1926 the name of the smallholding and mill was changed completely to become Llwyn Hywel, the name it carries today. I thought this was most odd, especially for an area like this, which is so entrenched in its own history and so keen to remember even tumbledown or indeed completely vanished houses and cottages by their long remembered original names. The name change was of course linked to the incident, as after it the mill house lay empty and eventually when new people came they must have changed its name, probably to expunge its treacherous connections with the events of 5 December 1925.

It was by all accounts a cold crisp Saturday night and the countryside was bathed in a silvery light from a frost-ringed full moon, a thin covering of powdery snow lay on the ground. Farm lads were enjoying a night out around the local pubs, and four of them were having a great old time down in the village of Whitemill. William Cethin Thomas and John Lewis were labourers at Alltygog Farm, (owned at the time by my husband's grandfather Robert Jones) and they were enjoying themselves with their friends William Owen and his brother John, who worked at Tanerdy farm further up the valley. William Cethin Thomas was in love, or possibly lust, with a pretty little maid who lived up at Llainddu mill, and as the lads supped up their beers they decided to take the circuitous route home and call in at the mill to see Lizzie. By the time they walked up from the village it was nearly eleven o'clock and when they arrived at the front yard of the mill they were surprised to see the old farmer and mill owner Thomas Richard Thomas, a big burly man, standing statue-like in his moonlit yard. Thomas was seventy-three at the time and contemporary additions to this tale have the old timer in love with Lizzie himself. Indeed, some embellish the story so far as to suggest that they were actually in bed together when the lads arrived at the mill! However, this seems unlikely, as both his wife and sister-in-law were present in the house at the time. For whatever reason

Farmer Thomas was justifiably displeased to have four rather inebriated young lads arrive on his yard unannounced at eleven o'clock on a Saturday night, and when he asked them what they wanted and they told him they wanted to see his maid Lizzie, he told them sharply that the girl was asleep in bed, and to get lost.

If only they had left it there, but feeling mischievously full of Dutch courage they taunted the old man as they left, and only went as far as the apple orchard where they hid for a few minutes and then went back down the hill to Llainddu Mill, determined now to see pretty Lizzie. Thomas went out again, this time he saw the men coming along the side of the wall by the mill building and then moving about near a pile of manure on the yard. He went inside again and this time he put one cartridge in his shotgun and then reappeared on the yard. One or two of the lads were smoking and he could see the red ends of the cigarettes as they inhaled. Thomas shouted at them to clear off or they'd regret it. They didn't go and as he raised his gun to fire a warning shot into the air the gun went off level with the men. The moon-bathed quietude was instantly shattered as the gunfire rang out echoing around these beautiful old hills. This was followed immediately by heart-rending screams as the young lads were hit by the pellets from the shotgun. They scattered like birds as they ran for their lives into the lanes. Three of the four were hit. William Cethin Thomas was the worst and as he ran he left large red spots of blood in the snow from the mill into the lanes. In the adrenalin rush and due to his youth and previous fitness the lad managed to run up the steep hill and into the lanes that led back towards Alltygog, but his injuries were so severe and his loss of blood so great that he soon collapsed groaning in the hedgerows near Penbryn Park farm. John Lewis, also hit and very scared, ran on without him to Alltygog. William Owen had himself passed out because of his injuries in the other lane that leads to Llanfihangel, and was being attended to by his uninjured brother John, who helped him home when he had recovered slightly. So poor William was alone, bleeding to death by the side of the road on that cold moonlit night. A farm servant from Rhiwfelin also making his way home found him shortly afterwards; he asked the lad if he was all right and he said he was. This man, called Edward Evans, could see that William was badly hurt and so ran to get help at Penbryn Park, and when the occupier Howell Evans and his two sons arrived back at the place where William was lying injured they could see in the light of the hurricane lamp they had brought with them that he was in a terrible state. William, bleeding profusely, tried to tell them what had happened, but he failed to do so and soon slid into unconsciousness. Howell Evans dispatched one son to get the police and the other to get Dr Alexander Lindsay from Nantgaredig. William died before the doctor could get to him, but his report to the court illuminates the tragic events well and tells how he found the body covered in blood, with copious frothing from the mouth and nostrils; it was still warm indicating very recent death. On examining the body he discovered a deep penetration wound just above the lad's left eyeball, there were huge swellings and the eyeball itself was hanging out of its socket, there was also a large hole in the side of the lad's neck. The post-mortem revealed that William had taken thirty-six pellets in his face and neck and some of the gun's discharge had entered his brain. Later, after PC Richard Davies of Cothi Bridge and PC David Davies of Abergwili had converged on the site and recorded the scene some transport was arranged to take the body to his mother and stepfather's house in Whitemill village. His body lay in pools of sticky haemorrhaged blood on the floor of the gambo as it made its way through the silvery-lit freezing lanes towards the village.

John Lewis, although hit in the head and neck too, managed to get back to his store-room bedroom in Alltygog, but was also discovered in a pool of blood later on when the police arrived at the farm to investigate the shooting. He was swiftly taken to the Infirmary where they managed to stabilize him. William Owen was also hit by pellets, but was not seriously hurt.

At 4 a.m. the next morning, Superintendent Peter Jones and Inspector Tim Hodge Lewis motored to the murder scene and then proceeded to Llanddu Mill. They immediately spotted the spent gun cartridge on the snow dusted ground in the yard, and saw clearly all the blood trails left by William as he had fled. The house was in complete darkness. They knocked, and a woman's voice was heard from an upstairs window asking who was there. 'Police' they said, and shortly after they saw the flicker of light in an upstairs bedroom. Thomas Richard Thomas appeared then at the front door in his nightgown, holding a candle. They asked him if he owned a gun, and when he replied to the affirmative they asked if they could see it. He showed them the weapon, and on examination of the gun they arrested Thomas. They took him by car to the County police station in Carmarthen, where he was charged with the murder of William Cethin Thomas. He went very quietly and with dignity it was reported. On the Monday morning he appeared at a special session of the Carmarthen Assizes Court, which was held in the vestry of Salem chapel in Whitemill, where he was said to be very pale, subdued and tremulous. He was wearing a great coat with a black velvet collar and a white silk muffler, he held his cap in his hands, and had difficulty following the proceedings as he seemed to be slightly dazed by what was happening. The report of that first hearing makes much of the fact that the accused was a highly respectable man, and tells how before retiring to the Annell valley some six years before he had been a successful grocer in the Rhondda valley, where he had been deacon of his chapel for nearly thirty-eight years. He was held on remand and transported from the court session to Swansea prison. The *Carmarthen Journal* newspaper report, which came out on 11 December, contained headlines and strap-lines that read: 'Midnight Tragedy at Farm', 'Sensational Affair' and 'Youth Shot Dead and Old Man Arrested'; yet it makes no mention of the mill owner's wife, after stating early on in the article that Thomas was a married man. Lizzie too is not referred to again in the report, once the love interest between her and William had been established, and one can only try and imagine how Thomas's wife, sister and the young maid coped with such a tragic scandal in a small community like this.

Thomas's charge was quite soon changed to manslaughter. I had been told by a former occupier of Llywn Hywel that he was found guilty and spent eleven years in prison. Eleven years in prison is a long time, especially for a man in his seventies, and I wondered if Thomas had actually survived his sentence. I expected a straightforward answer to my query, either he had survived or he had died in prison. However, the prison record book, now lodged in the archive department of Swansea's County Hall, revealed a different story. The book showed a charge of 'Murder' written in pencil against Thomas's name but there was no sign of his sentence length or date of discharge or even his death. Intrigued now by the case I decided to check again in the press around two dates which looked like trial dates that were lodged next to his name and prison number in the record book. Sure enough the case was heard again and finally went before a jury who, to my astonishment found the old timer 'Not Guilty.' There were several reasons for their verdict it seems but the main one centred on his advanced age and his hitherto unblemished

Christian character. Additionally, Thomas had said from the start that he had had no intention of wounding let alone killing anyone, he was just an old man rather frightened by the intrusion of four young men late at night, he also said that he was very hard of hearing and hadn't heard them ask to see his maid, he just thought they were up to wicked mischief at his place.

I believe the incident occurred for a number of reasons and perhaps the most relevant is that Thomas was *not* local, he didn't know these boys, he didn't know their families and they didn't know him either except that he was a newcomer. Added to that he was not a Welsh speaker, and if he had been perhaps the boys would have left him alone when he asked them to. I am a relative newcomer here myself and I know that nearly eighty years on this is still a hard community to crack!

'Impressive Scenes at Victims Funeral' reported *The Welshman* newspaper on 18 December 1925. By all accounts young William's funeral was a very sad affair. Large crowds attended and Salem chapel at Whitemill was full. The article says the mourners both inside the chapel and outside in the village sang beautifully *O frynaiau Caersalem,* and it notes the poignancy of the inscription on the wreath William's mother and stepfather bore; it read, 'We do not know what pain he bore/ We never saw him die/We only know he went away/ And never said 'Goodbye'. It is perhaps little wonder that Thomas auctioned the mill a few months later. It was bought by a man called John Rhydderch from Cwmllydan-isaf in Llanllawddog.

The old name of my house was lost then, along with Thomas himself, as he seems to have disappeared into thin air as soon as he was released from prison. However, on 5 December every year from now on we think about those tipsy farm lads and the awful

No. 29 Nominal Register. (9336—4-7-06)

Register Number.	Name: Surname.	Name: Christian Name.	Summary Convictions, Debtors, Courts Martial &c.: Date and Place of Committal. 191 .	Re-examination and Trial: Date and Place of Committal. 191 .	Assizes and Sessions.: Date and Place of Conviction. 191 .	Offence.	Sentence.	Education.	Age, Height, and Colour of Hair.	Trade or Occupation.	Religion and Birth Place.
1485	Evans	Herbert	5.12.25 Pembroke Dock			Wil. damage	1 Mon. Imp. or £4.10	1	19½ 5-4 L. Br.	Soldier	C of E Wrexham
	4th Dec. 1925										
1486	Morgan	Timothy	5.12.25 4.12.25 Aberystwyth Boro			Drunk & dis.	14 dys. H.L. from 5/12/25	2	25 5-3 L. Br.	Stoker	C of E Carmarthen
1487	Davies	Daniel Morgan	5.12.25 4.12.25 Aberystwyth			Refusing to work in Union	4 dys. H.L. from 5/12/25	1	35 5-2½ D. Br.	Lab.	C of E Rhondda Valley
1488	Thomas	Thomas Richard		4.12.25 Carmarthen Co. Rem. 14.12.25 " 22.12.25 Trial. Assizes [illegible]		Murder		2	43 5-8½ Grey	Farmer	Independent Carmarthen
1489	Cooksey	James	12.10.25 4.12.25 Port Talbot Co.			Com. Assault	21 dys. Imp. or £2.2	2	31 5-6 Lt. Br.	Collier	C of E [illegible]

Entry of Richard Thomas's murder charge in the nominal register, 1925.

consequences of their foolishness, and we will wonder why the mill owner, the respected septuagenarian chapel-goer and former deacon, did such a rash thing on that moonlit night so many years ago. My husband and I have planted a few crocus bulbs in the hedgerow where William died. We paced the one hundred yards back towards Llanfihangel from Penbryn Park gate, which is mentioned in one of the court reports to be the actual spot of the lad's death, and as we did so we thought of them all and felt sorry for their anguish.

Dr Caroline Jones.

Carmarthen Gaol

Carmarthen Gaol, which was completed in1792, was one of three county gaols built between 1789 and 1796, the other two being in Cardiganshire and Herefordshire. The building itself occupied the site of the old castle, and attracted much interest, especially from the gentry, even before its construction. Why was it built? The prison reformer John Howard's second visit to Carmarthen Gaol, on its old site in 1788, and his subsequent report, which criticises the conditions inside the prison, prompted demands for rebuilding.

Carmarthen was already undergoing redevelopment and improvement, and because it was the oldest town in the principality, the gaol was a rather conspicuous building. Its design was rather distinctive, and perhaps this is why there was so much interest in its architecture, and its architect, John Nash. Nash's personal and professional lives have both been under close scrutiny. He arrived in Wales in 1785, and indeed it was architecture that attracted him. He began his career in Wales after responding to an advertisement he saw in 1785 that sought helpers to restore the roof of the parish church, St Peter's; it was during the following year that Nash came up with plans for the gaol in Carmarthen.

The plan of the so called 'ideal' prison was thought up by John Howard in 1777, about twenty years after he had been convinced that something in the way prisons were currently being designed had to change. The design he favoured became known as 'Howardian', and it was a style perused by Nash. Essentially, this meant that the prisoners were segregated, with separate courts, around which would be wards for the different types of prisoners. The chapel was central to the prison. Howard intended for each prisoner to have his/her own individual cell. This was in keeping with Howard ideology that segregation was the only way to reform a prisoner. To Howard solitude was the key. However, with the ending of transportation in 1792, total segregation was not totally achievable, as the prison began to fill up with prisoners who could no longer be carried off to American colonies. Transportation had previously been a more effective way of dealing with criminals.

Of course, it cost money to keep people in prison, and perhaps it was this way that conditions were unacceptable for such a long time and why overcrowding was tolerated. Sometimes whole families would be sharing a cell, and yet the problem of overcrowding was not totally unsolvable, the spread of gaol did much to control the problem.

Nash's design for Carmarthen Gaol was rather dispersed. Segregation was carried out where possible, and the different classes of prisoners, felons etc. were kept separate, with night and day cells. Any kind of communication between prisoners was forbidden. The use of hoods meant that every prisoner maintained anonymity during group activities, and when attending chapel the prisoners were screened off from one another, and were kept in separate boxes so they could not even see each other. The building itself would have been made of brick and would have been well ventilated, something that was slowly becoming a common feature of British prisons. Carmarthen prison was then a new

Carmarthen Gaol, 1900.

building, yet it was contained within the walls of the old castle. This would have made the prison façade rather imposing to an outsider. This was not accidental, and, indeed the façade was designed to act as a deterrent, and its location meant that every person living in Carmarthen would most likely have passed by it at some point. It was not a building that was meant to be hidden. It was a grim reminder of the consequences of unlawful behaviour, and it was hoped that fear would be instilled into people to prevent them from falling into a life of crime.

Normally, the design of institutions for this period centred around the 'U', 'E' and 'H' format, still in use today, and a typical example of the 'H' block in Northern Ireland. Nash appears to have deviated in respect to Carmarthen Gaol, possibly because his design had to fit into a comparatively small area, within the boundaries of the old castle.

The actual conditions inside the prison were a reflection of how society viewed the criminal. This goes some way to explaining how the prison system developed the way it has. There was a great emphasis placed on location, and prisons were built to ensure that this was a prominent feature. Apart from the actual danger of infection from disease due to previous poor ventilation, there was also the fear from society of the possible contagion of criminality itself. It was believed that cleaner air would prevent the spread of disease, and criminal behaviour was not exception. It appears that the Victorians really did believe in the notion that cleanliness was next to godliness. It was a tool used in the fight against crime, as though higher levels of hygiene in the prisons would somehow act as a moral cleaner on the inmates, perhaps serving to inspire them to reform themselves. This was one of the main purposes of the prison in the first place, after all.

So what was daily life like for the inmates of Carmarthen Gaol? The best sources for this are the diaries of the prison governors, and were written by governors such as John Westlake and George Stephens. These are very interesting insofar as they gave us a real insight into the prisoner's day, and what comes across most strongly is the sheer monotony of it. According to these diaries, which date from 1845-50, the prisoners attended chapel every day. These diaries are quite detailed and comprise essentially exactly who came into custody each day, and why. It would appear as though there was an acute need to control the poor and the working classes, who were seen as a threat to people and property. This was done in a number of ways. The practices of picking oakum and working the thread wheel by prisoners were central to the prison regime, although the use to the thread wheel was seen as controversial, mainly because of the physical effects on some prisoners. The thread wheel was said to 'aggravate pulmonary and rheumatic complaints, as well as causing varicose swelling and severe weight loss.'[1] Sheer exhaustion would no doubt have been the result of the estimated 7200ft each prisoner would have climbed every day, approximately. The prisoners would have found these punishments monotonous, tiresome, and it was hoped that they would serve to prevent them from re-offending, since it was the mind as well as the body that was being punished. A typical entry from the governor's diaries reads something like this: 'The prisoners attended chapel and school and the remainder of the day employed at the wheel and picking oakum'. The work they would have been expected to do would have involved tasks such as 'painting the house of correction.' The routine was very much the same, day-in, day-out. This routine was applied to the prisoner's diet, which certainly had no variety; bread was eaten with every meal.

These diaries also show how religion, along with education, was a tool used to combat crime. It was widely excepted that a lack of religious and moral teaching in a prisoner's life was a major contributing factor for their demise into crime, and so making the prisoners attend chapel every day, it was hoped, would encourage them to reform themselves. Every day in Carmarthen prison was a fixed routine of physical work, schooling and religious teaching.

What was the typical prisoner like in Carmarthen Gaol? We can find the answer to this in *Felon's Register*, an important document as it contains over 1400 entries of criminals coming into Carmarthen Gaol between the years 1844-1871. One of the most important features of the document is that it gives us a picture of what the 'typical prisoner' was like. On average, it would seem the typical prisoner was male, rather small in stature, largely uneducated and descended from the working class. He would have most probably been viewed as an outsider in society, as this was the accepted image of the typical criminal. Between the years 1878-1924 the most frequent crime tried was theft, and this was not just in Carmarthen, it was true across the country. As a result the working class were generally seen as a threat to society, and the poor, it seemed, needed to be controlled – prison was seen as the best way of doing this.

The doors finally closed in March 1922, when the Home Office decided that Swansea prison would serve the needs of the area. The home office made the decision to close the prison, along with eight others, in an effort to

Spilman Street and Old County Gaol.

'affect economies in the national expenditure as urged in the *Geddes Report*. The building itself was to be demolished in 1935, according to the *Carmarthen Journal*, in order to make way for newer county buildings to be constructed on the site of the old prison.

Rebecca I. John.

Stranger than fiction

While waiting to take possession of Castell Draenog, a run-down farm and farmhouse that was to be our new home, we'd been invited to stay with friends in their especially grand farm house.

They too were starting out on the farming ladder, but their farm was a part of the one time Abbey estate and their farmhouse was Whitland Abbey House, one of the many mansions built by an affluent nineteenth-century business man.

I won't labour the point, but it is not hard to visualize that they were starting further up the farming ladder, or on a better quality ladder than my poor young wife and I.

For a short time we occupied the east wing of the grand house, which overlooked the River Gronwy, and a small meadow with its kingfishers and the herons that stood sentinel on the riverbank. On the far side of the river was an ancient woodland and as morning dawned it came alive with a chorus of song.

What with the river and its woodland backcloth it was a heavenly setting. Nevertheless it was claimed by local people that the old Abbey remains, separated by the narrow country road from the mansion, were haunted.

One night Allan, our young farmer friend, and I were returning home to the Abbey and as we were approaching the drive entrance to the mansion, we saw someone crossing the road from the old Abbey ruins.

Apart from the sound of the wind blowing in the trees, a Tawny owl hooting and fleeting glances of the full moon appearing between the scurrying clouds, there was nothing else to distract us, or anything unusual to arouse our suspicions… other than the person that crossed the road!

On entering the house and seeing his wife, Allan's first reaction was to ask her what she was doing out on the road. She simply replied, 'Why do you ask?' adding, 'I'm not likely to go out of the house on my own any night let alone on a windy night like tonight.'

Turning to me and somewhat mystified he mumbled, 'Somebody was out there!'

I had to agree, we most certainly saw somebody or something! But who would be out in the country, miles from anywhere, on a miserable night when no sensible man or beast would even consider venturing out of his hide or home?!

We were both newcomers to the district and it was some time later that I heard the story of farmers travelling along the Llanboidy to Whitland road by horse and cart, and finding that their horses would stop by the ancient Abbey, and having to be urged on. Incredibly it appeared that horses always stopped at the place where we saw our apparition (or whatever?) Local people claim that it is the ghost of the 'White Lady' of the Abbey!

It is recorded that notable Princes and Chieftains of the twelfth and thirteenth century were laid to rest in the Abbey's hallowed grounds. It is said that it was once considered to be Wales' most sacred sanctuary, equating in a ecclesiastical sense to Westminster Abbey.

The long-standing story of the 'White Lady', the Abbey ghost, set me thinking! There was of course Gwenllian, the daughter of Prince Rhys. She had been brought from Dryslwyn and was buried near the Abbey's 'High Altar'.

Then there was also Janet, the daughter of 'Nicholas of Carmarthen'. They were the only women that I can find relating to the Abbey's past.

Unfortunately the Abbey's records were either destroyed or for some perverse motive removed from the Abbey. It is claimed that the *Black Book of Carmarthen* was a product of Carmarthen Priory but it is also suggested that the *Black Book* was produced in part if not in total by the monks of Whitland Abbey. Sadly today, only a part of the Abbey's history can be gleaned.

While the legend of the 'White Lady' persists, I question whether the apparition is of necessity a woman?

Why not Dom Henry Vaughan who was fatally stabbed in the Abbey's cloisters? It must have been a pretty black deed, especially as it was committed by another so judged holy man who it is claimed came from Neath Abbey!

In the middle of the thirteenth century it is claimed that the Abbey was partially destroyed when it was attacked by a force of three thousand horse soldiers.

No mention is made of the bloodshed and the number of monks that were killed.

In the early part of the fourteenth century it is recorded that the Black Death struck Whitland Abbey, but again there is no mention of dead monks, yet following the Black Death, in the Abbey's Poll Tax Return only seven monks are recorded as living in Abbey!

There are stories of Whitland Abbey monks going off to the crusades, and of warring Abbots fighting in different parts of the principality. Most certainly the Abbey wasn't always a haven of peace-loving brother monks and it makes you wonder just how holy some of the incumbents really were!

Whatever the Abbey's historic past and the tales that have existed for countless years may tell, I only offer the locally held belief that someone's spirit still roams and haunts the now peaceful ruins and that they believe it is the 'White Lady', whoever she might be!

I can only honestly say what I saw!

David L. Jones.

On a sultry afternoon at haunted Aberglasney

It was one hazy summer's afternoon during the time Aberglasney slept its long sleep shrouded in unkempt solitude under a spell woven of weeds. A bumblebee lightly droned its restrained cello note across the strings of long grass. All, so it seemed, languished in warm decadent idleness.

What was it, exactly, that was disturbed that day when half a dozen student nurses waded boisterously waist deep through the undergrowth towards the house on another of their Sunday afternoon escapades? For it is not only in the dead of night that strange things stir.

One of the intruders that day was destined to make a name for himself as a singer and actor. Geraint Griffith recalls that as the place was so large they decided to explore it in pairs. It was 1969 and much of the mansion's interior remained accessible. Geraint and his companion (now dead) ventured upstairs and to the upper floor. In one of two lavatories they found a very fine Victorian water closet which, though they appreciated its aesthetic qualities was, naturally, the cause of juvenile amusement when they saw that it bore the name of its inventor: 'Crapper'!

Curious as to whether there might be a similar utensil in the adjoining lavatory, Geraint attempted to open that adjoining door, but it was firmly closed. Noticing a little sign indicating it was 'engaged', innate good manners prompted him to apologise. They both wandered down the corridor and seeing nothing of interest soon returned. The second lavatory door was now slightly ajar, its indicator signifying that it was vacant. Indeed it was completely so, its contents apparently long since plundered. Like that notorious figure of fiction on his return home one fateful Christmas Eve, Geraint too 'did pause, with a moment's irresolution... and did look cautiously behind the door. There was no means whatever of locking it, which puzzled rather than alarmed them'.

Becoming aware of a tolling bell close by, as they thought, they went to a window overlooking the cloister garden. Directly below them there were two figures moving casually across the long grass. A man and a child. The surviving witness has no recollection of the child's dress (possibly because it made no impression at the time), but the adult's clothing was striking in its oddity. Especially so considering the weather that day. He wore a long cloak of coarse brown cloth reaching to the ground and a peculiar hat with a wide brim and a rounded crown similar to a Cardinal's.

Neither of the observers spoke but immediate unstated inquisitiveness caused them to go down at once to see who these unusual visitors might be. On the first floor corridor they met their friends who had not seen anyone. They were soon outside in the garden but there was no one there. It would have been necessary for the persons they had seen to run in order to be out of sight before the young people emerged from the house. There was no one and the bell was silent. The two on the upper floor were the only ones who saw or heard anything untoward.

Time out of mind Aberglasney has been a palace of many mysteries. The seemingly sunny harmony of the present belies its brooding and bedevilled past. For there is still something there in the shadows that adulterates its ancient peace. Something that intensifies the deepest shadows when night comes, but that can make itself known on the loveliest of summer days... still.

Today, fair-weather visitors and their

The driveway to Aberglasney.

carefree companions captivated by its resurgent bloom, may be forgiven for imagining idyllic and privileged bygone pleasures. In truth, such halcyon days were all but banished from Aberglasney for the past hundred years by heartbreak and distress. Joy and delight at long intervals have tugged briefly but in vain at its mantle of gloom. The opening years of the last century knew gaiety and radiance just as assertive as that of the present, but it is a place where widow's weeds soon overshadow a bridal gown. *Et in Arcadia ego.*

Following the untimely death of her husband in 1907 at the beginning of a promising new period in the history of the house, the heiress, Mrs Mary Anne Emily Jane Mayhew, went into reclusive exile in the Norfolk Hotel, South Kensington. Aberglasney was again forlorn and unoccupied as it has been several times in its long history. It drowsed in catatonic unease, furnished and habitable yet deserted and virtually neglected. There are those who would say it was not wholly at peace. Once in a while it was excitedly whispered that its châtelaine was about to return. The mansion's shroud of dustsheets would be shaken, its grounds groomed. But no one came. One decade decayed into another until the sombre eve of war over thirty years later when the long awaited lady returned at last from London. Her coffin lay in state in the Great Hall.

These sullen circumstances thus invested a place already deeply imbued with a longstanding and sinister reputation, with the *sine qua non* of the archetypal haunted house. A fearful curiosity to be gazed upon in fascination from a safe distance.

Schoolchildren would venture there sometimes on a matinée visit, running through the yew-avenue and tiptoeing for a closer look at the windows of the dreaded Blue Room.

During one such adventure the late Miss Ren Rees of Broad Oak recalled that at the critical moment a clap of thunder rent the sky and a door slammed or a window fell violently as a sash-cord broke. Whichever, they fled in terror as fast as their little legs could carry them.

By the 1930s it was commonly referred to as 'Plas yr Ysbrydion' (the phantoms' mansion) according to the late Reverend Ifonwy Hughes Thomas, a well-known rambler (in the pedestrian sense!), who was one of a constant stream of visitors. Its custodian told him that here, erstwhile, had been one of the most beautiful gardens in Wales. On that occasion in 1933, however, the dandelion and its cronies reigned prodigally and despotically over all. But was there any truth in the rumour that it was haunted, the young visitor wanted to know? Had its keeper ever encountered any of the visitants responsible for Aberglasney's infamy?

'Yes', he answered quietly, 'once at dusk in 1912. I was standing at the front of the house when I saw a tall man dressed in black walking slowly towards me; then, when he was almost by me, he vanished …'

Some blame a tragedy of long ago. Several maids suffocated in that upper chamber known as the Blue Room. A seventeenth-century contemporary recorded that strange lights, colloquially called 'corpse candles', presaged the awful event and, although its fateful venue has rotted into oblivion, whatever happened within it became heavily imprinted on Aberglasney's very existence. Stouthearted men who dared keep vigil in that room would flee in wide-eyed terror fortified though they were with mulled liquor and other futile precautions.

A curse hangs over Aberglasney, so legend says, brought upon it by a wicked squire who wilfully cut down a sacred tree that had drawn the pious and curious in unwelcome numbers to trespass on his land. Whatever truth the tradition embodies, strange to relate, it has menaced and intimidated the fearless and gallant even in our enlightened age.

What of the silent figure Geraint Griffiths and his companion saw in the grounds that summer's day, when all around was in a state of forgetfulness? Unbeknown to the witnesses it bore a remarkable resemblance to the *Nobilis in Anglia* (English nobleman) illustrated by Abraham de Bruyn in 1581. No history of costumes reproduces anything else which fits their description so perfectly. To which, of course, some would respond that it does nothing to dispel yet another of Aberglasney's many enigmas. Early on a Sunday evening, the knell may well have been that of the bell of nearby Llangathen church calling the faithful to Evensong. Conceivably a fellow student may mischievously have held that latrine door, though none of them had previous knowledge of the house. The whole illustrates Aberglasney's ability insidiously to unnerve one, always leaving an unresolved question. In this instance who *did* walk with them that hazy afternoon?

J. Towen Jones.

7 Special People and Places

Llanpumsaint parish church

Llanpumsaint is a growing village in a leafy North Carmarthenshire valley, which is dominated by its parish church.

The church was built during the sixth century by five saints. They were Gwyn, Gwyno, Gwynoro, Celynin and Ceitho. In the church, behind the altar, oak panelling stands in tribute to them.

The five saints were five brothers. It is said that they were quintuplets born to the wife of Cynyr (Farfwyn) Uarodrwch. The family originated from the parish of Cynwyl Gaeo, in the far reaches of the North Carmarthenshire hills.

An old legend stated that they slept with a stone underneath their heads in the caves of Dolaucothi, until the return of King Arthur or until a truly Apostolic Bishop came to occupy the throne of St David.

Sometime during the sixth century and prior to the building of the church, a Christian missionary named Seion joined the five saints on a preaching mission around the countryside. But, whilst travelling across the hills south of Llangeler, Seion was struck by illness and he died and was buried. A memorial stone was erected for him and to this day, the place has been known as 'Llechseion', the stone of Seion.

The old chronicles are rather hazy as to the exact origin of the church. One of the chronicles, however, states that the five saints and their followers came together on a set day, and after praying to God to make known to them the spot on which they were to build their church, they threw a hammer. It fell on a field called 'Moelfryn', on a farm situated to the north of the village. There they began to build their edifice.

Unfortunately, everything appeared to go against them; the wagons were continually breaking down and the oxen and the men they employed were dying. Due to these difficulties, the five saints came together again to pray and to throw the hammer. It fell this time near a Druidical Temple that was located in the neighbouring valley, and there they built the church, which they named 'Llanpumsaint', the Church of the Five Saints.

It was alleged that a well, called 'Ffynnonbumsaint', on a nearby farm was the well that serviced the church.

In the churchyard, on the left hand side of the footpath, near the entrance to the vestry, stands an ogam stone. It looks just like any ordinary stone, but engraved on one side of the stone, is a cross inside a circle. Ogam was a form of writing, which was devised by the celts. It is said that this ogam stone belonged to the old building, the Druidical Temple.

The church was restored, virtually rebuilt by 1882. It was during Canon Joseph Lloyd's period of incumbency. Middleton and Sone, Westminster and Cheltenham carried out the restoration work. Previously the church had a gallery at the west end, which was approached from the outside by a flight of stone steps and a door in the west wall. All these were removed in 1882. The west wall was almost rebuilt, the vestry was built, the west door was replaced

Outside the church, the east side.

with a new one and the bellcote at the west end was rebuilt.

Until 1862 the day school was held in the gallery of the church. The pupils had to pay a weekly fee for their education. Many children came from poor family backgrounds and so could not afford to go to school. These children had to go without education.

In 1888, a stone building was built adjoining the churchyard, for keeping biers, coal, firewood and other articles belonging to the church and it served also as a stable for the horses of people coming from a distance to attend the services of the church.

During the year 1932, the church was extended to the size that it is today. The extension work was carried out to the west-side of the church, by Mr Ralph Fry, Kingsbury Episcopi, Somerset with Mr W.D. Caroe, Westminster, as the architect.

Present at the re-opening service was the Bishop, The Right Reverend David Lewis Prosser; The Archdeacon, the Venerable Robert Williams, M.A.; the Rural Dean, Reverend Evan Jones, B.D., Llangain and Reverend John Herbert, a former vicar of Llanllawddog. In the evening appropriate sermons were delivered by the Reverend T.C.

The Ogam Stone.

The old church before the insertion of the East window.

Phillips, MA, St David's Diocesan Missioner and the Reverend Talog, Davies, MA., Curate of Llangeler.

Before 1932, the main door was located in the west wall. Evergreen trees sheltered the doorway. At this time there wasn't a window in the west wall or the east wall either.

The east window is a memorial to Canon Joseph Lloyd and his wife Mary. Canon Lloyd was the incumbent of the church from 1877 to 1920. Their son, Canon Walter Lloyd, commissioned a new east window for the church in memory of his parents. He chose Mildred Eldridge to design the window. Mildred Eldridge was married to R.S. Thomas, the poet, who was a curate in Canon Walter Lloyd's own parish. Mildred Eldridge chose to design the window with Mary in the centre, Joseph on the left side and a young woman or an angel on the right side. The design is based on the fact that the vicar's name was Joseph and his wife's name was Mary. The east window was dedicated in August 1939.

The west memorial is a memorial to Reverend Joshua Jones and his wife Elizabeth Louise. Reverend Jones was the vicar of Llanpumsaint parish from 1920 until 1944. The window was dedicated during December 1963.

A section of the old church, which is still in existence today, is the Leper's window. The small window is located in the north wall, the chancel, near to the altar.

One of the numerous gravestones in the churchyard is a memorial to Martha Llwyd, a

The East window.

hymnist who was buried there in 1845. Martha Llwyd was born Martha Williams in 1766 on a farm called Natbendigiad, in the parish of Cynwyl Elfed, on the outskirts of the parish of Llanpumsaint. What little education she received is believed to have been of the religious nature.

She was united in matrimony with David Lloyd on the 30 December 1785 when Martha was aged nineteen years. Evidence that supported the fact that she was illiterate was that she signed the marriage register with an 'X', in lieu of her name.

They spent their entire married life in a house called 'Glanyrafon' in the centre of the village. There they raised nine children.

Buried with her husband, who predeceased her in 1844, their grave is located beneath the yew tress on the north side of the church.

During the early years of the last century, the customs of the church and its people were different to what they are today. Even so, the difference was not that much greater to the present day, a century later.

There was a Communion service in the morning, once a month, every month. On the following Sunday, in the afternoon, there was an evensong service and those who had not taken communion on the previous Sunday were required to remain behind at the church in order to receive their communion after the evensong service. Therefore, every member of the church had the opportunity to take communion once a month.

The church bell was rung fifteen minutes prior to the beginning of the service and it was a second time when it was time for the service to commence. Of course, in those days, everyone walked to church except for two or three families who travelled by horse and cart. During the month of June it was customary to hold annual meetings in the church, with food being served in the schoolhouse. For all the services, there would be a large congregation and the chancel area

The Leper's window.

The west side as it is today.

The West Window.

of the church was where the children were seated. The schoolchildren had a holiday that day.

Three ladies from the church joined together to give the food and they carried all the crockery, teacloths and all the other essential items they required, from their homes, in large baskets. After the morning service, there would be tea, bread and butter and cheese served, all of which were homemade. Later on came the cream cheese, which was a luxury for the children as at home they only had farm cheese. For the afternoon tea, there would be a cake on the table.

Due to the onset of the First World War in 1914 and subsequent scarceness of food during the war, the tea had to come to an end although the services were continued.

There was an occasion when a funeral cortege came to the church at Llanpumsaint from a farm near Llanllawddog. Many people walked to meet the cortege and by the time the cortege reached the church, there would be a multitude of people following a procession behind the coffin.

Everybody walked, as was the custom at the time. They used to carry the coffin for a long distance, and the carpenter would then change the bearers often if there were only a few present, as would often be the case if a poor person was being buried or if all the farmers were busy with the harvest.

The village subsequently used a horse-drawn hearse, which was last used during the early 1950s. A horse-drawn carriage was also available for wedding services in the village. If there was a wedding in the church, the bride and her father along with the bridesmaids would travel to the church by horse and carriage. At the time it was not customary for the bride's mother to attend the wedding service. She would be at home preparing the reception. One wedding tradition would be that the best man would throw money to the children and one of the boys would be given a shilling for holding on to the reins of the horse, for the duration of the wedding service.

Now in the twenty-first century the population of the village is steadily rising whereas the congregation of the church is dwindling. Traditions have changed, very few people, only its neighbours, walk to church. The majority of the people travel by car. A century ago the church would have probably been nearly full for a Sunday service of worship. Now, you would be lucky to fill five or six pews.

Pamela Jones.

A fairly substantial farm

Built of local stones, with a slate roof, Abernawmor is a classic West Wales farmhouse near Gwyddgrug and Pencader in north Carmarthenshire. From the west, the house shows three sash windows on the upper floor, and two on the lower with a front door between. When we moved in on the last day of 1976, it had been empty for some years. There was electricity but no running water or sewage. There was no identifiable garden or boundary: cattle, and especially sheep grazed up to the front and back doors. As well as a family home, in the last quarter-century the house has been, for me, an icon of social and local history.

Around 1916, thirty years after the house was built, an ancient axe-head was unearthed by a farmer ploughing about half a mile away. The axe is evidence of human activity more than 3,000 years ago. The earliest local people probably arrived from western sea routes up to 2,000 years earlier. These pioneers, using stone tools to hunt and clear land for cultivation, must have made comparatively slow progress from what is now Pembrokeshire, towards local landmarks now known as the river Teifi and Mynydd Llanllwni. Whoever left a stone axe behind in the lower Teifi valley had probably been exploring woodlands, from a camp, if not a settlement, nearby.

The nearest Bronze Age *crugiau* are characteristically on higher ground than this house, but closer than the buried axe-head, there's evidence of an Iron Age Celtic fortress, Castell Craig y Banc. Unexcavated, one of about sixty Iron Age forts in Carmarthenshire, this is now part of Banc Farm, Pencader. An earthwork around a few acres, it was probably built around 200 BC. By then, perhaps, the weather was colder and wetter than in the Bronze Age. Slash-and-burn farming techniques may have exhausted soil-fertility, making division of land and defence of settlements an inevitable part of human life. Settled life was now based in recognisable agriculture, supplemented with hunting and fishing. People used horses and dogs for hunting and herding. They lived in wattle-and-clay houses, thatched with heather. Shepherds and herdsmen used rough summer shelters during summer grazing on the moors, beginning each year at the Mayday festival. The end of this season, when the animals were taken in for the winter, was on 1 November. When we first lived here, farmers still sometimes moved their cattle indoors or to lower pasture

Abernawmor from the west, 1977.

by 1 November, perhaps evidence of unbroken tradition.

Only the local chief and his family probably lived in the fort or *castell*, while the whole community used it as a refuge when necessary. Close-knit extended families lived on the products of farming: milk, cheese, butter, meat, barley and oats. There were fish in the rivers, hares in the clearings and birds in the air. Since living here we're been the lucky recipients of sewin caught just below the house, a hare and ducks shot just above it, by men who learnt their skills as youngsters.

The next big cultural change after the Celts was the Roman occupation. Carmarthen, capital of the *Demetae* people, was one of two Roman cities in Wales. Romans probably walked or marched between Carmarthen and Caernarfon along a ridgeway-route, already ancient, known as Sarn Helen. Less than a mile from here, the Roman road is near the present A 485 Carmarthen-Lampeter road at New Inn. This settlement round a junction of ancient routes has been known as Spital, which suggests a Roman hospital. Farming, hunting and fishing continued to sustain local people through the occupation. Roman civilisation as such was largely confined to towns and roads, but new trading opportunities must have made some families and settlements more prosperous.

When the Roman legions withdrew, the Teifi valley became a disputed frontier between Goedelic Celts to the south and Brythonic in Ceredigion. Brythonic rule was imposed in about 500 CE. From then onwards, for perhaps another 500 years, the Welsh language and script gained over Irish and Ogham. This half-millennium also included The Age of Saints, when David and his followers established Christianity, suppressing the 'devilish' old religion now known as paganism. By 850 CE, Pencader and Gwyddgrug were part of the *cymwyd* or commote of Mabudryd, part of the south Wales kingdom of Deheubarth. Outside the farms and settlements, the countryside 'was still densely forested, and inhabited by deer, boars, hares, wolves, martens, foxes, and probably bears.'* This made the area remote from good transport links, and defendable by native kings or princes of Deheubarth, who knew their way around. Even by the twelfth century, the journalist Geraldus Cambrensis

Abernawmor from the east, 1977.

wrote 'The Welsh live not in towns or villages or forts but as hermits they frequent the woods.'

In the two centuries between the Norman invasion and the death of the last native prince Llywelyn Olaf in 1282, west Wales was a battleground, with local kings or princes fighting Normans and their allies. Near the middle of present-day Pencader, and visible from just below this house, is the site of a motte and bailey castle, built in about 1145 for the Norman lord Gilbert de Clare. This was a wooden stockade on a great mound of stone and earth, with a bailey including kitchens, barns, stables, sleeping quarters and maybe a chapel. It was scarcely finished before it was burnt to the ground by a local army led by three sons of Gruffydd ap Rhys, reclaiming what was by now the capital of Mabudryd. In 1156, two of the brothers repaired the castle to be a base for their own invasion of Ceredigion.

Abernawmor from the north, 1977.

William the Conqueror's great grandson became Henry II, King of England, in 1154. On his way to becoming a great European monarch, Henry needed to settle the rebellious Welsh kings or princes. In 1157 he did a deal with Rhys ap Gruffydd, the youngest of the brothers who had taken Pencader Castle. The agreement was soon broken, and in the fighting that followed, Rhys became Lord Rhys, sole ruler of south Wales. In the spring of 1163, Henry's army marched unopposed across south Wales till they reached Mabudryd, where Rhys, advised by his uncle, finally submitted to Henry. Twenty-five years later Geraldus Cambrensis wrote the story of an encounter between Henry and an Old Man of Pencader.

The story passed into folklore, commemorated on a slate memorial beside the main road in Pencader, between this house and the old post office.

By the fourteenth century, Abernawmor was named as a settlement in the Grange of Gwyddgrug, given by Lord Rhys to the Abbey of Talyllychau –Talley. The description of the Grange in the 1324 Inspeximus Charter of Edward II is one of the earliest references to local place-names still used. Within the Grange of Gwyddgrug 'white robed monks from Talley Abbey acted as parish priests and collected the rents and other taxes from the tenants of the small farms.' There were taxes on marriage and inheritance, an annual tax of seventeen sheep and seventeen lambs, and a portion of grain, which must only be ground at the grange mill.

In this system where sexual morality, family, money and religion were bound up together, monasteries became very prosperous. By the time Henry VIII sacked them in 1534, Gwyddgrug grange and its mill were valued at £6-16s-8d: the most valuable grange of the abbey. The Talley lands, already run by a lay steward on behalf of the Abbey, now became a manor under the crown. Farmers and other tenants still had to pay rents and taxes. Unusually, local tenancies passed to the youngest son 'as customary heir' could be inherited by the youngest daughter if there was no son. In 1633 'John Griffith holdeth by lease one tenement with appurtenancies called Tir abernawmor to the yearly rent of 9s payable at the feasts aforesaid.' Legally a tenement is a permanent holding of some kind, and the mention of appurtenancies suggests the right to graze animals, collect wood, draw water and so on: Abernawmor in 1633 was an established farm. The house might have been made of stone, thatched with straw, but many houses were still made of earth, straw and dung. There may have been a loft for sleeping, and a separate parlour and kitchen, but it was almost bound to have been draughty, smoky and cold in winter. Clothes were made of wool or leather, and shoes of wood or leather. This house in winter is sometimes an island in a sea of mud. When we first lived here, Luther the clog-man still had a stall in Carmarthen market. We bought wellington boots from him, but thick wooden clogs that could be rinsed or brushed were also practical footwear.

By the eighteenth century, local people were still farming, hunting, and trading in produce, still paying rent, taxes and tithes, but they didn't all go to church on Sundays. In 1710, a visitor examining the state of the church in Wales reported that sometimes 'between two and three hundred hearers' listened to an unlicensed trainee Presbyterian preacher, in a meeting house near the church in Pencader. The meeting-house, built partly of stones taken from church property, was perhaps more 'decent' than the church. These were 'generally in a nasty condition ' at that time. Eventually more people went to local chapels, at New Inn, Gwyddgrug or Pencader, than to church. The fact that chapel-going families were obliged by law to pay tithes, or church tax, as well as maintaining their chapels, was perceived as great injustice and eventually led to Welsh dis-establishment in the early twentieth century.

At the end of the eighteenth century David Griffith, farmer, lived at Abernawmor with his beloved wife Catharine. Their sons were David and John, their daughters Mary, Rachel, Elizabeth and Sarah. In February 1793, David Griffith was 'sick in body' when he wrote his last will and testament, now preserved at the

National Library in Aberystwyth. The will gives a precious glimpse of a large and loving family. David Griffith left the remaining unexpired lease of Abernawmor to Catharine and youngest daughter Sarah. The other children, some at least adult by now, were to receive three pounds in 'lawful British coin' on Catharine's death. There was also a cupboard for David. Grandsons William and John were to have five shillings each, and William would also have a yearling heifer.

Also in the National Library is an early nineteenth-century ledger from the Rees shop at New Inn. The Travellers' Rest, which gave the village its modern name, was near the crossroads of the Carmarthen-Lampeter road and the drovers route over the mountain to Brechfa and Llandovery. It was already an ancient junction by the time Thomas Rees of Llanllawddog set up shop in the eighteenth century. The Rees business grew, providing trading opportunities, employment and apprenticeships.

The National Library's great ledger details transactions for twelve years from 1812, when many people came to New Inn to buy or sell butter and other goods. One account shows that William Williams of Abernawmor sold calves, butter and a yearling filly.

This was around the time of successive bad harvests, followed by the Napoleonic Wars. The Welsh Land Commission later reported that war with Napoleon had made the rich richer and the poor paupers. Social security in Wales and England came from each parish looking after its own, through the Parish Vestry. Local Overseers of the Poor collected a tax and gave the proceeds in cash, food, fuel or clothes to those in need who could prove their local right. Others were forcibly evicted from the parish. The Pencader Vestry Book shows that in 1800, forty-seven local people received cash or barley. By 1819, there were 147 paupers, including those with trades:

Abernawmor from the west, 1999.

shoemaker, tailor, carpenter and smith. A single mother, Anna, lived rough with her child. In 1822, ninety-two paupers were listed, one of them John Daniel, tenant of Abernawmor, an eighty acre farm. Soon the demand for local farmers, already impoverished, to pay tolls when taking their animals or produce to market, inspired the Rebecca Riots.

Houses and farms were still not grouped together in villages but stood singly in well-chosen locations. Abernawmor, for instance, is close to the meeting place of two small rivers, and protected from the worst of the north and east winds by the rise of land towards Mynydd Llanllwni. Like neighbouring farms Glanawmor and Banc, it's marked on the 1840 tithe map. Of the two buildings shown, I can see the possible remains of one, grassed over, from the window as I write. Part of the other building was used as a house till this was built in 1888.

The railway made this area comparatively prosperous in the second half of the nineteenth century. The first train arrived in Pencader in June 1864, and prospects for trading perishable produce such as milk, butter, and meat improved immediately. The effect of the railway on the local woollen industry was even more dramatic. The first of a new generation of mechanized spinning mills was built at Sunny Hill, two fields from here, in 1870. The railway station and junction, mills, other factories, houses, schools and streets built around the turn of the nineteenth and twentieth centuries largely shaped the present day villages.

By 1902, Abernawmor was 'an exceptionally nice farm with dwelling-house, barn, stable, cow-house, cart-house and three good pigsties.' With nearly eighty acres and the right of water from Sunnyhill factory, the farm was one of nineteen adjoining lots for sale by auction at the Porth Hotel. Whatever the outcome of the auction, it was 1906 before the farm was bought by its tenant, Rees Davies, from the owner Courtney Cecil Mansel, Baronet, of Maesycrugiau, for £1,310. The house's twentieth-century history deserves at least an essay of its own. The comparative prosperity that finally enabled tenant farmers to buy their farms a century ago didn't last much beyond the Great War. Abernawmor farm was sold to Blaenblodau in the 1950s. The house was rented to a local family for a few years but was then empty for more than a decade. It was largely weatherproof, there was a mid-twentieth century fireplace and curtains at the windows, but by the mid-seventies, ceilings and chimneys were collapsing. One of the pleasures of living at Abernawmor has been to meet people who lived here as children or youngsters, and others who remember helping with the harvest. We were lucky enough to arrive when hay was still made into 'small bales', and privileged to give our neighbours small help in return for great hospitality and conversation. We began to learn where we'd come to live, and stay.

*Quotations and historical information from *This Small Corner,* a history of Pencader and District by Steve Dubé, Carmarthenshire County Council, 2000.

Janet Dube.

Rees Davies (1867-1953) Fellow of the Institute of Builders

Prize-winning entry

Rees Davies was the youngest of eight children from Llanstephan, who attended Llanybri Primary school and the only one of the family to cross the estuary to attend a Dame school to further his education. He trained to be a master builder and married Ann Parry of Llanstephan, daughter of a master mariner.

Mr Davies lived in Carmarthen most of his life and was one of the best-known figures in the town and district and he was held in high esteem. In his younger days he served on the executive committee of the Y.M.C.A (the present Carmarthen Library) and campaigned for local Temperance reform. He became Senior Magistrate of Carmarthen Borough, chairman of the Carmarthen Division Liberal Association and senior deacon for forty-five years of the English Baptist church. He was also one of the founder members of Carmarthen Rotary Club.

As builder and contractor, Rees Davies was responsible for erecting a range of buildings. I list some of his projects below:

The new wing of the County Infirmary (Priory Street), the Broadcast Hall (now the Parry Theatre) at Trinity College, opened by the Duke of Kent and other extensions there, including tutor's houses in Pentremeurig Road, factories for dried milk products at Carmarthen and Merlin's Bridge, Haverfordwest, the headmaster's house at Pibwrlwyd, nos 6 and 7 Penllwyn Park, Parcmaen Street, Job's Well Road, Myrddin Crescent. Cae Glâs House (Monument Hill) – where he died, the row of cottages at the base of Monument Hill (by traffic lights), 'Ucheldir', now the site of the old Model school, the bandstand and grandstand, Carmarthen Park, the brick works at Dolgwili, with two kilns, (which eventually closed because they ran out of clay), the old Midland Bank, Lammas Street – his proudest achievement, and the architecture of this building for which he was greatly admired.

He also owned part of the Wellfield Estate and did some building there. His offices were in Catherine Street, near the old Model school.

K.F. EMPLOYERS' LIABILITY INSURANCE. DOMESTIC SERVANTS. A 12

THE
OCEAN ACCIDENT & GUARANTEE CORPORATION,
LIMITED.
36 TO 44, MOORGATE STREET,
LONDON, E.C. 2.

Workmen's Compensation Act.
Domestic Servants.

Renewal Date 11th February 1919 191

AGENT'S DEBIT NOTE.

Workmen's Compensation, Act, 1906: Domestic Servants.

Policy No.	Name and Address of Assured.	Schedule.	Rates.	Premium.	
073516	Rees Davies, Model Villa, Carmarthen.	Indoor Servant		5	0

TOTAL PREMIUM £ 5 0

Agent's Debit Note, 1919.

Oil portrait of Rees Davies, now in the possession of his grandson Stephen Rees Davies in Australia.

The contract for installing electricity was given to Charles Chapman of Blue Street, who married Rees Davies' daughter Dorothy (Dora). Gas was provided by private companies before it was nationalised and sited in Morfa lane, where Tovali and MFI are now. His other daughter Eleanor (Nell) married Professor Cuthbert Colin Davies, an Oxford Don.

His secretary for forty years was Miss Owen of Picton Place. Mr Meredith Williams was office manager and his daughter-in-law Fran Williams still lives in Morley Street. He is still remembered as having a forbidding appearance and was always dressed in breeches and leggings. The late S.I. Evans worked for him and Mr Noel Collins' grandfather William Thomas Rogers (d. April 1941) formerly of 'Brookwood', No. 66 Parcmaen Street was employed by him as a master plumber. Mr Wilkins of 'Eryl House', College Road a

The band stand, Carmarthen park.

forebear of Mr Henry Wilkins (Clothier – Hall Street) was the mason. Mr Ravenhill who lived in 30 Parcmaen Street and died last year was also a plumber in his employ. His widow lives in Lime Grove Avenue.

Rees Davies' son Victor Parry Davies with his great friend Cliff Jones (of Owen Jones shoe shop family) joined the navy in the First World War, and his father paid for him to become a midshipman.

After the war he settled in Melbourne, Australia and married Clarice Ann Farquhar of Queensland. They had three children, Gwynne (of Wellfield Road), Malcolm Rees Davies, who died in a Naval accident in 1948 and Stephen Rees Davies who was born in Carmarthen in 1939.

In 1932, Victor returned from Australia where there was a severe recession at the time, to help his father establish a laundry in Priory Street (the site of Denzil Evans garage). Victor was first of all trained in laundry work in the Savoy Hotel, London and was later employed in the Second World War, to decontaminate clothing after gas attack. Mr Bill Davies of Ty Rhys knew Victor very well and remembers him playing football for the town.

Mention has been made of a Mr L. Crabbe, who lived Myrddin Crescent, who worked as his architect and surveyor.

However the architect for the Parry Theatre (Broadcast Hall) in Trinity College was Mr H. L. Harby, a one time neighbour of ours in the tutors houses, who was Head of Handwork in

Farrer Birmingham

Quote for 6 No 286 Tubs in Series
also Single 2 Flanged Ends in Straw & White
No Pedestals Rees Davies

Llewellyn Merchants Pembroke Dock
Quote today certain for 12 thousand
20 x 10 Sea green Slates Old Sarnau Station
Rees Davies

Paint Darwen
Send today urgent 2. 14 pounds No
28 Water Paint Rees Davies

Memo in Rhy Davies's hand.

The Carmarthen Steam Laundry,
Dyeing & Cleaning Works, Ltd.

Works: PRIORY STREET. CARMARTHEN. Offices: 33 ST. CATHERINE STREET

High Class Family Laundry.
Families waited upon in Town and Country.
Your patronage is earnestly solicited.
Price Lists and other information upon application to the Manageress.
Telephone 64. Telegrams—Carmarthen Laundry.

REES DAVIES,
BUILDER & CONTRACTOR,
CARMARTHEN.

Building materials of all kinds in stock.
Joinery work of every description made to suit customers requirements.
Machine made Mortar supplied & delivered.
Haulage work undertaken to all parts by Mann's Steam Tipping Lorry.
Agent for the celebrated RUFOID & SLATEX compositions, and the well-known Ruberoid Roofings and Dampcourses.
Telephone— No. 48 Carmarthen. Telegrams— Rees Davies Carmarthen.

Advertisment in the District Official Guide, 1932.

the college, where he taught many useful skills to his tutors. He was also a qualified architect and credit was given to him for designing 'The Wing' later named the Dewi Hostel, the craft building and the remodelling of the College Chapel between 1933 and 1943.

Both these houses were built by Rees Davies in around 1900 (fin-de-siécle) as commodious family dwelling houses of style and character. Latterly bow windows were added to No. 6, while No. 7 had at one time a window, now bricked up, in the attic.

No .6 (Redholme) and No. 7 (Llwynon), Penllwyn Park.

Extract together with adverts from a Carmarthen booklet – 'District Official Guide, published by Vickery Kyrle and Co Ltd 4 Great Malborough Street, London.

Rees Davies Builder and Contractor, 'This firm is very well known throughout the whole district. Many large contracts have been undertaken in South Wales and successfully carried out. Mr Davies has had life-long experience in the trade, and can always be relied on to place his valuable services before all enquiries. This firm enjoys, and deservedly so, the confidence of a large clientele.'

Marion Davies.

The Gwilli Railway

My husband and I first discovered The Gwili Railway Preservation Society and Gwili Railway in 1988 when driving through Bronwydd. I had assumed the railway would be the usual narrow gauge tourist attraction and had a delightful surprise when I found full-size coaches pulled by a superbly robust steam engine. I remember clambering on board and feeling transported back in time to

Number 7 Penllwyn Park.

the 1950s. The carriage was almost identical to those I remembered when I was a child and travelled from Seacombe, Wallasey, Wirral to Wrexham, North Wales for the monthly horse sales. In 1988 The Gwili Railway only went as far as Llwyfan Cerrig and all too soon the Gwili steam locomotive arrived at the station and we got off to stretch our legs and explore the picnic area. When we returned to Bronwydd station we browsed around the station shop before crossing back over the line to the car park. A sign advertising refreshments stood alongside a stationary buffet carriage. We drank freshly made tea and homemade cake while I mentally placed Gwili Railway at the top of places to show family and friends who came to stay.

I have been back many times during the past fourteen years and the steam and the noises from engine and whistle still cause a childish buzz of excitement. Each time I go I cannot help but be impressed by the dedicated work done by the team of volunteers who run and maintain the railway. The track has been extended northward and now terminates at the new Danycoed Station instead of Llwyfan Cerrig. Just in time for the 2002 Easter Bank Holiday, a toilet block was completed at Llwyfan Cerrig. This is undoubtedly a comfort to those who like my husband and myself have left middle age behind. It will also enable us to stay at Llwyfan Cerrig for longer and make greater use of the picnic area when we are accompanied by our youngest grandchildren.

Our two eldest grandchildren are now teenagers and while they have enjoyed the Santa Specials over the years, they considered themselves too grown up to join us at Easter 2002 for Thomas the Tank Engine. I have a sneaking suspicion that they were disappointed that I had taken them at their word and not included them in the party. We booked for the Saturday and were blessed with just the right weather for a grand day out. Our party included three small boys who clearly thought they had been magically transported to the Island of Sodor. The girls, two-year-old Caitlin and nine-year-old Charlotte, may not have had quite the same interest in Thomas but they were equally as pleased as the boys to celebrate the Fat Controller's birthday, shake hands with the cow and ride on the miniature railway. Everyone participating in the event, from the coach drivers ferrying passengers between Pibwr-lwyd car park and Bronwydd Station to the staff serving refreshments at Llwyfan Cerrig were good humoured and helpful. I have nothing but praise for all the volunteers who make all these occasions so special.

Volunteers are always needed at the Gwili Railway. You don't need to have a burning desire to drive a steam train; there are multitudes of ways in which anyone can join in and help. You don't have to make a regular commitment, even a day or a few hours at one of the many special events would help the hard-pressed regulars. A great deal of maintenance and renovation is done when the railway is closed to passengers. (My husband and I know this because we became members and spent several weekends doing a photography project. Every time we went, in fine weather or in foul, there would be a band of volunteers beavering away with tools or paintbrushes.) The volunteers hail from all walks of life. Some are, or have been, employed on national rail networks, others have backgrounds in engineering; accounting; teaching; some are retired; some are still at school.

This once defunct railway makes a unique contribution to the area, not only as an attraction but also for its sense of community.

The sidings, where the volunteers restore rolling stock.

The bridge beyond Danycoed, which is awaiting the day when it can carry the Gwili Railway to Line to Conwyl Elfed.

Looking towards Carmarthen, the ultimate southerly destination for the Gwili Railway.

The Gwili Railway Preservation Society has a lot to be proud of. It is thanks to the committee, all the volunteers and those who have supported it in other ways during the past twenty-five years that future generations may, some day in the future, see a steam engine puffing between Carmarthen and Conwyl Elfed Station, or even Llanpumpsaint, if visions become realities.

Jenny White.

The Temperance Hall

At the beginning of the century the Band of Hope movement flourished. The aim of the movement was to dissuade people from partaking of the 'demon drink,' and to encourage drunkards to 'dash from their lips the cup that ensnared them.'

At that time, there were two taverns in the village of Llangathen, one was known as 'The Star', whilst the other was known as 'The Three Compasses.' The latter adjoined the churchyard, and was said to be well patronised by the toilers of the land.

One day, Colonel Mayhew of the Royal Welsh Fusiliers, who was the local squire and lived at Aberglasney Mansion, became an ardent supporter of the Band of Hope. In his zeal, he was among the first to sign the pledge and denounce the pernicious evil of drink. Such was his enthusiasm that the Colonel decided to erect a Temperance Hall in the village. The building was situated in a prime position that overlooked the grounds of Aberglasney Mansion, and on looking through the large bay windows, the enchanting panorama of Grongar Hill unfolded before one's very eyes.

To add further charm to the Temperance Hall, inscriptions in Gothic script were placed on the fascia boards. The inscriptions embodied the doctrines of the temperance movement and read, 'Let us not Sleep,' 'Watch and be sober' and 'Yfwch fyth diod gref.' To the searching eye, the faded lettering can be seen today as reminders of a bygone age.

The mock Tudor Hall was built by a builder who lived in the nearby Bath House, once the watering and wash place of Bishop Rudd of Aberglasney. In 1905 the cost involved in building the Temperance Hall waqs £1000 and this was borne in full by Colonel Mayhew.

One fine feature of the building was the domed clock tower. The clock was decorated with coloured mosaics depicting the national emblems of Wales, i.e. the leek and the fleur-de-lys. The clock struck on the quarter and was wound once a week. Such was the accuracy and reliability of the clock that it became a byword among the farmers and roadmen that worked within the confines of the leafy lanes of Llangathen.

Idris Davies.

MEMBER'S CARD

This is to Certify that

Kate Jones

BECAME A MEMBER OF THE

Llangathen & District

BAND OF HOPE

Dec. 12th G. A. Mayhew

1904. Secretary or Registrar

I PROMISE TO ABSTAIN FROM ALL INTOXICATING DRINKS AS BEVERAGES

Band of Hope member's card, 1904.